The Country Property Buyer's Guide

A complete guide for buying, financing,

developing, and living on rural property

Garry Cooper

The Country Property Buyer's Guide

Copyright © 2013 by Garry Cooper

Table of Contents

Section I

How to Find and

Buy Country Property

Section I — How to Find and Buy Country Property

Prelude

This book will take you for a relaxing stroll through the world of buying and developing country property, and will enlighten you with some truly helpful information and hints on financing country property, as well as give you an in-depth understanding of what living in the country is all about. I say "stroll" because this book is not a technical manual on contracts or financing and such. It is written so that when you finish each section, you will come away with a profound understanding of the fundamental considerations of each aspect of your country property purchase, development, and lifestyle with ease.

I have not only lived in the country my whole life, I have a bachelor of science in business administration, have been a real estate broker for over thirty years, and have been developing bare land into country home sites for nearly forty years. You will "stroll" with me as though you were just on a country walk all the way through this book, learning something new and enlightening at every step. By the end, you will realize that you have just learned some of the most valuable lessons available on this subject matter, in a way that is clear and easy to understand. Best of all, this information is all in one source! You will find that all the information you learn here will also be valuable when you become a seller of country property someday.

As we stroll along, you will learn how to protect and guard yourself from legal pitfalls, learn all about "country etiquette" so you can be a good neighbor, and also learn the many ways to save money whether you are negotiating on the property or developing it into your own Garden of Eden!

Some of the things we will be exploring in this book are:

- What to consider when buying country property.
- How to locate property that fits your needs and desires.
- The most critical factors of evaluating rural property.
- The huge differences in financing country property and bare land over in-town property.
- Negotiating and legally protecting yourself when purchasing your dream property.
- The key factors and techniques for developing country property, which will save you thousands of dollars.
- How to be a good rural neighbor, which is often the source of many bad experiences.
- Some truly helpful tips on country living, including advice on fencing, livestock, tools, septic systems, and wells.
- What emergency supplies you should keep on hand.

…and many other great useful tips on country living.

I consider the financing of country property to be the trickiest and the most important aspect of the buying process. Pay particular attention to that section, as it will greatly influence your success at purchasing your dream property. I am not going to bore you with a bunch of numbers and financial data; I am just going to familiarize you with some key concepts and techniques that are essential to grasp so that your property-buying process is as easy and productive as possible. I have seen folks in my forty-year real estate career waste decades of time by not understanding basic country property financing concepts, which I lay out for you here.

I want you to keep in mind that I am not an attorney, and I am not giving legal advice in this book, even though I mention things from time to time that have to do with contracts and the law. Every state is different, and laws change often; you should consult an attorney for any legal questions and advice concerning real estate in your state. I am just making general legal references to make you aware of some of the issues that can arise when you are buying or selling country property.

With these basics, you will have a sound foundation for buying, developing, and living your country lifestyle dream on your own little piece of our planet! Enjoy.

— *Garry Cooper*

When You Move to the Country, Start by Asking Yourself "Why?"
Why Is the Reason I Want to Move to the Country Iimportant?

Typically, when you consider moving to the country and to a rural lifestyle, it is for one or a few of several reasons. Some folks just want privacy from their neighbors and the hustle-bustle of city life. Others have a dream of owning horses or raising livestock, or even becoming self-sufficient. Perhaps you want to raise a commercial garden for the local farmers' market or breed livestock for income. Maybe you just want to find a spot where you can listen to the creek flow by or look over a canyon or valley or some other panoramic vista in your retirement years.

In any case, the reasons that are influencing your decision to move to the country will, or should, determine what kind of property you are looking for. For the person who is looking for a place to grow crops, a rocky or steep property will prove to be very impractical. Soil conditions, water availability, a flat terrain, and perhaps a location close to the market will factor into selecting the ideal location. These locales are typically in valleys or flat ridge tops, depending on the options available and that person's other priorities. For instance, this same person may want to be near a creek or waterway, may desire a distant view, or may want to move far enough away to cut down on visits from acquaintances or family. Any number of factors will come into play when formulating where the best spot to buy property is. For this reason, it is important that you and your family take an organized approach to lay out the reasons for your move to the country.

You should start by making a list of the reasons why you yearn to move to the country. It may sound like an unnecessary task, but it allows your entire family to weigh in with their thoughts and concerns on making such a move. Then, each reason should be prioritized and agreed upon by those in the decision-making process so everyone's concerns, wants, and needs are clear. When you do make a move to the country, you want your entire family's experience to be a positive one. If you don't think this is an important step, consider the following as an example of where this approach can help you.

Let's say you want to move to the country so you can enjoy living on a creek where you can fish and swim from your own property, let the kids raise some hogs for 4-H, and have a little elbow room from the neighbors. Sounds simple, doesn't it? Then the kids ask how they will get to school, and you let them know that it is only about a forty-minute bus trip each way, which with all the stops is not out of the ordinary. Then they ask how they are going to get to their Boy Scout meetings after school on Wednesdays, football practice five days a week, and their friends' houses on the weekends. Now there is a huge wrench in the plan, and you are just getting started.

With a slight inquiry on line, you find that the only creekfront property you can afford is even farther from town than where Mom or Dad wants to live, or is in an area known for drugs or violence. Here again, the entire equation changes, and you will find that taking an organized approach to picking what type of country property you are looking for will be more valuable than you realize. You can now cross the creek off your list, as well as those properties that are too far to be practical, given your family's lifestyle. Now, you are tempering your dreams with practicality, which is key to having a good country property living experience. As time goes along and you get more information about the areas, costs of properties in various locations, and the various features available, as well as a better understanding of your family's thoughts, that perfect country property will begin to take focus.

Don't Forget to Consider These Important Factors in Your Thinking!

In evaluating what type of property and which locations might work for you, you will need to consider some other factors that you might not have thought of before. I will lay out a few of these for your consideration here, but your life's circumstances may bring many other factors into play that I or the next person can't even imagine.

We touched on some of the issues pertaining to the needs of children, but even adults will have factors that will influence their property-buying decisions, and teen kids will bring other thoughts to the forefront.

The commute is a factor to be considered by all. Not only are you running the kids around and becoming their taxi, you will need to drive back and forth to work; you'll run out of milk, beer, tobacco, or toilet paper sooner or later; and your guests will have to drive to see you at your home. Moving to the country will cause you to see much less of those that you see now, which might be a blessing, but not always. You may have an elderly relative or friend that you check in on or a coffee group that you meet in the mornings. You may be working on a quilt or other project with a friend. You may need dialysis or other medical needs or be at an age and point in your overall health where being closer to medical facilities is a good idea. You may just want to work out at the club every morning and evening. These are all considerations you might make, along with the cost of gasoline and other vehicle costs. If you have teens that are just beginning to drive, you will want to consider that many rural roads are narrow, curved, not graded properly, and are somewhat dangerous for the inexperienced driver. I moved from a canyon I loved to near my daughter's high school based much upon this factor. The period of time you plan to stay at a property is also an important consideration.

Your planned use of the property is another key issue that requires further thought. You may be planning to have a dog-boarding kennel or horse-boarding facility, to sell produce or some product from your land, open a yoga clinic or spiritual center, build a shop and manufacture custom furniture, or establish some other similar use, such as a bed and breakfast. You need to know that every county or jurisdiction has different rules for such activities, and it is typically allowed only in certain "zones," as set forth in the county's zoning ordinances and general plan. Many activities may be allowed in many different zones, but they might also require a special use permit, which is granted only after a public vetting process. You can understand how putting in a stable or dog kennel would cause much more noise, traffic, and other issues that might not be acceptable in certain areas or not allowed if opposed by the neighbors. It is always a great idea to swing by the county office and check with them on the permitted uses of the property you are considering, along with inquiring about any known water, septic or sewer, or other important issues that they might be aware of. **You should never buy bare land without doing this under any circumstance.**

You also need to consider the suitability of the property for your intended use from a practical point of view. If you intend to grow cherries, check with the agricultural commissioner, local college, or other such sources to determine the suitability of the area for such crops. Often, you will notice what trees and crops are thriving in the area in the neighbors' yards that are similar to the property you are considering. Check on the soil conditions, water availability, and any known pests in the area, such as deer and insects, and do a little homework so you have the best success. If you plan to raise sheep or other livestock, consider the fencing practicality and costs along with the predator situation in the area. You may not want to build a fence on property full of ravines or with solid rock just four inches under the surface! This isn't rocket science; just take a good objective look around in light of your delineated needs.

Consider the costs associated with developing the property that you are considering. For instance, the farther away you are from town, the longer it takes to get concrete trucks, lumber trucks, and your construction workers to the property, which all adds substantially to costs. Choosing land that is solid rock or needs a bridge for access are both costly features, as are many other property development factors. You can get a better idea of these factors later in this book under the property development section.

I have touched on a couple of factors that are often overlooked in the quest to find your very own "Eden," but in the following portion of this section, I will elaborate on some of the major considerations that I have seen come into play in my experience.

The Neighborhood Should Be One of Your Top Considerations!

First, and what I consider foremost, when finding the right country property (after you have determined your particular needs) is the neighborhood. This is not to say that there are not other key factors, such as water and power availability, which I will examine later in this book, but without a good neighborhood for your purposes, your country living experience can become a nightmare.

Generally, there are good and bad areas in about every location, but there are some general rules that seem to ring true in all of them. As an example, I have found that the farther out and away from services you get, the more "un-tame" the folks living there are. This is not to say that all folks away from town are *Deliverance*-type lunatics, or that some of the best folks on the planet don't reside there, but in general, I have found this to be true. In the more remote places, there are often a lot of folks that choose to remain unemployed or are unemployable due to their felonious past, and find that cutting firewood for the locals or doing handyman work or some other less-moral activities are the best ways for them to survive. The "druggie" proportion of the folks in these areas is typically much higher than in the closer-in areas as well. You will find that there are many more non-code living structures, camp trailers being used as permanent homes, and other inexpensive living quarters in these areas. Typically, these areas do not appraise adequately when the owners try to finance a structure, which contributes further to this lower-end housing situation. If you are the rugged type, want inexpensive land, and are able to handle your own security needs (as the police often have over an hour's response time), this may be the area for you. To each his own, and in my younger days, I probably would have been in heaven!

Once you buy in a neighborhood, you are part of it. The factors that contribute to its character are unlikely to change during your lifetime, or at least for a long time, so don't expect anything to change. Your resale value will be directly affected by the quality of your neighborhood, and for this reason, it is of the utmost importance that you *never* overimprove, which is developing your property beyond what is typical for the neighborhood. Usually, all the fine construction you do, that great horse setup with lighted arenas, or other costly improvements you make will not be investments you can recover if they are not typical of what is already found in your neighborhood. This is the one mistake I have seen made more times than I can count, and one that, as a real estate broker, is a pill to hand out that is never welcome. It is important that you really keep this concept at heart when you are shopping for bare land or buying improved rural property.

As a matter of fact, this factor often leads to great opportunities for a buyer to buy a property that has all of his or her desired improvements at a greatly discounted price, and at much less than you can build them for, so keep this in mind. I don't just mean buying in a remote, "sketchy" area, but in any neighborhood. For instance, you might find a property with a pool and tennis court in a nice area where such improvements are rare and only typically found on properties out of your price range at a price where these improvements are basically being gotten for free! This is where shopping comes into play.

One of the best ways to choose a neighborhood is to visit it often and drive it, and even walk it. See if the folks take care of their properties, typically have the things you want in a property, and don't keep junk cars and debris in their yards. If you are planning to build a home or plan on buying a home, look for areas that have on-site constructed "stick-built" homes, as opposed to mobile or modular-type homes. If you have children, look for children in the area and take the time to meet some folks in the neighborhood and "feel" them out. Check into the school district, as this one factor has a huge affect on property values and desirability. Areas that have community organizations, such as historical societies, community-improvement groups, and such typically contribute to having a solid neighborhood that will have a tendency to improve rather than decline in quality. Talking with the neighbors of an area also can be critical in learning of issues facing the area, such as fire protection, planned developments, flood risks, environmental concerns, or other factors that might affect the desirability of a property in that area for your needs. Folks working on their yards on the weekends can be a highly valuable source of information about an area, and they are usually delighted to talk about their neighborhood. If you find they are not friendly, that alone may be a red flag for the area.

However, if you are looking at a particular piece of property and you meet the neighbors, take care not to over-rely on what they have to say. They may want to scare you away so their brother can buy the property or may withhold some key information, such as a chemical contamination or bad well, just so they can get you as a neighbor because you seem normal or sane to them. You should always meet the neighbors of any piece of property you are considering for a number of reasons, but just keep this thought in the back of your mind.

I will also mention that any property that is near a landfill, especially on a road to it, is not as desirable due to the traffic and especially the litter that is generated. If you are close to it or "downstream" of it, this may be a concern for possible groundwater contamination, and the aroma begins to come into play. Again, I can't stress enough the importance of evaluating and choosing your neighborhood carefully when buying country property.

Some of the other factors that you might want to consider are the general flora and fauna of the area, your sun exposure, whether the roads and drives are paved, how the access is in the snow and high water, what the access is to riding trails for horses or ATVs, and what areas are good and safe for walking and riding bikes.

As far as the flora and fauna go, you may find that you fall in love with the majestic pine trees or a scenic bluff that your potential home is nestled in or below. Then, once you move in, you find that this bluff blocks all of your winter's scarce sun and that the only thing that will grow in the shade of the big conifers is mushrooms from your deck and mold in your closets! This may float your boat, but I would be nutty in a matter of one winter (think *The Shining* with Jack Nicholson). I know folks who live in the dark of California's giant redwoods among the ferns, mushrooms, and molds and wouldn't have it any other way! I personally must have a far-off panoramic view with great winter sun exposure.

You also have to keep in mind that some areas are prone to wildfires. My dad, who was somewhat of a pyromaniac, lit a good one on his land (and the neighbors') back in Ohio in the woods in the dead of winter. In California, the foothills below the pine and conifer altitude and above the valley floors are known as "chaparral." This eco-niche includes occasional wildfires as part of its natural lifecycle, and some of the seeds of indigenous plants that grow in this chaparral area are unable to germinate unless they are seared by a wildfire! This chaparral area has benefits of being above the mosquito habitat and has much better views and sun exposure than the conifer forested areas, but you must take great care in clearing the brush and trees from around your house and outbuildings due to this fire risk.

Something else you must consider when thinking about the plants in various areas is their toxicity. Many areas have poison oak, poison ivy, poison sumac, or some other plants that may irritate you if you are sensitive to them or their pollen. My family is mostly immune to poison oak, which is thick out here in California, but I have friends who get huge one-inch-high blisters on any part of their body from touching the plant, or even from where a dog rubbed against them that had been in it. Trust me, if you live in areas that have such plants that you are sensitive to and you have dogs, you are in for it! Also, be aware that many areas have many different types of plants with stickers. We have goat-heads here, which are a vine that grows flat and unnoticeable on the ground until you or your child has stepped into them with gusto, at which time your feet are filled with tiny goat-head-shaped nodules. Your impulse is to sit down to relieve the pain of the stickers pushing into your feet, but if you do, you will usually be sitting in more stickers. Then we have the usual wild black berries, stinging nettles, and thistle. This is just something else to keep in mind but shouldn't be a deal killer, as if you are a sissy, you don't need to be looking at country property anyway!

The fauna, or wildlife, is also a factor you may want to mull over. I love most wildlife, including foxes, skunks, coons, deer, and such. However, I can do without the mountain lions, bears, and poisonous snakes! You may also have to contend with mosquitoes and ticks on both you and your animals as well. When I lived in the foothill area, the mountain lions killed my sheep, and we killed a lot of rattlesnakes around the house—seventeen one year! Once we thinned them out, we would only kill a snake or two a year. I still loved living in that area, and if not for the treacherous road and my daughters moving towards their driving years, I would probably still be living there.

If you are planning to raise chickens or turkeys, the foxes and coons will wipe you out if you don't close them up at night. Designing your pen right is essential, and we will talk about that later. Rabbits can wreak havoc on your garden and landscaping as well, so we will discuss this further in the livestock and fencing sections.

Living on a creek or river brings with it its own major concerns. While nothing may be nicer than living on a nice creek or stream, they carry risks and costs that you should be aware of. Creeks are there to carry water from the higher areas. Every one of them can become a raging whitewater, rising many feet above normal in a matter of hours, if not minutes. The government will usually set a 100-year floodplain as a point of reference for building and for flood-insurance purposes. This is the height that the water will reach typically only once in every hundred years. However, this does not mean that it will not happen two years in a row, or that a flood event that might happen only every five hundred years will come along. For that matter, you might experience a flood of biblical proportions during your ownership that no one would expect and that no construction will withstand. You are fore-warned.

I lived on a beautiful creek and bought some other properties in my neighborhood to develop. We got a huge snowstorm over Christmas in the hills and mountains above us, and the snow line dropped to an unusually low altitude. Then, a huge warm tropical rainstorm came in and dumped several inches of rain on our already-saturated ground for several days. This warm storm melted the snow for thousands of feet in elevation, and when combined with the unrelenting rainfall, our usually three-foot-deep creek turned into a fifteen-foot raging river that washed out almost every bridge on it. My neighbors and I were then living on an island until we could replace a major portion of our bridge at great expense. The water eroded my creek frontage and made some of my land drop enormously in value. Luckily, our home was well above the flood and was not at risk, but my neighbors weren't so lucky. Some had their homes flooded, and their furni-ture and hot tubs were drifting rapidly by as we watched. Some of the creekfront homes had the earth eroded under their foundations, making them unsafe to occupy. To make things worse, after the flood, one of the county bridges on the main road was hit with a tractor being hauled home on a truck from some neighbor cleaning his flood-damaged lot, and the entire bridge fell into the water, leaving hundreds stranded. Never underestimate the power and destructive potential of any waterway on, near, or on the way to your property.

You can buy flood insurance, and the cost depends on where the height of your floor sits in relation to the 100-year floodplain. The farther out you are from the flood plain, the less that it costs, but you will most likely have to have a licensed engineer issue a "flood elevation certificate" to establish just where the floor is. This is not particularly cheap, either, and will run from several hundred dollars to several thousand, depending on several factors. Most lenders will require flood insurance in order for you to get a loan from them if you are within one of the designated 100-year floodplain areas, and any insurance agent can give you some idea of this cost prior to you making a decision to purchase a particular piece of property.

Snow presents its own challenges to country gentlemen and women. The more rural roads have less priority for the snowplows. If you live on a privately maintained road, you and your neighbors are on your own to clear the snow, and you alone are responsible for your own driveway. Also, as you will come to learn in the section on road-maintenance agreements, you might not get help when you need it to clear this snow. Some country folks find themselves making it a point to leave their cars out near the paved county road where they can plan to have some access to work and back if their private roads and drives become impassible. If you live in a snow area, and you are developing your own lot or buying a home that already exists, you will want to keep this in mind. I have friends who are fine with being snowed in for days at a time, but they either work out of their houses or are retired.

When you move to the country, you may find yourself tending to live on a gravel road. In this case, plan on not having a clean car like you did when you lived in the city. During the winter months, you will have mud, and during the summer, you will have dust. Your tires and shocks will wear at a slightly faster pace, and you will have to drive a little slower than you might be accustomed. If you live near a gravel road where traffic runs past your home, inevitably the neighbors or their guests will speed past and stir up dust. Keep this in mind when you are buying, as this dust finds its way throughout your entire house no matter what you do. Often folks will put up a "Slow, Dust" sign, which just means the dust builds in your house at a slightly slower rate! It is best to live a hundred or so yards from any such road. If you are a clean car type person, don't even consider buying property on a gravel road, as it will drive you insane.

If you like to ride horses or ATVs, walk, or you or the kids plan to ride bikes, you will want to look for an area that is friendly to these. This is especially true with bikes and kids, as many rural properties have narrow winding and hilly roads that present a hazard to kids and anyone walking or riding bikes. Some areas have nice straight and wide roads with big shoulders, and some actually have pedestrian and equestrian routes near them. Other properties might be on the edge of government property with forestry roads and trails that are nothing less than excellent for off-road activities and horseback riding. If any of these activities are at the top of your priority list, keep an eye out for that property that is friendly to them.

Remember, too, that you might want to check on garbage service, Internet availability, and mail facilities when you are shopping for property in the country, as often these items that you take for granted in town could be much different than when you move to the country!

What If I Have a Road or Driveway That Is Shared with the Other Neighbors?

Sharing a road with neighbors when you move out into the country is not an uncommon thing. Many of the roads are gravel and quite often need more gravel on them or need to be graded to get the potholes out of them, or could even have a major problem like your mutual hundred-thousand-dollar bridge getting destroyed by a flood, which actually happened to yours truly! I won't kid you, any time you share a road—or share anything with a neighbor—you are going to have some degree of problems, and someone on it is going to find some justification not to pay their share or simply will not have the funds to do so. With a private bridge, most of you might not have the funds to repair or replace it, and this becomes a real nightmare.

When roads need repair is somewhat of a subjective judgment—which often depends on how nice of a car the neighbor making this judgment is. It is typically everyone's responsibility to share in those costs. The basis for this legal principal is one that has been in place through common law that was accepted and adopted in most states from the times when we were a territory of England. After all, it is equitable and fair. However, if someone doesn't pay their fair share, it is usually not financially advisable (or practical and advisable from a neighborly point of view) to take legal action to enforce that law. Oftentimes, there is a "road-maintenance agreement" that is signed by all the neighbors that spells out each person's responsibilities. Usually, from what I have seen, these do nothing more than reiterate what is each person's responsibility under common law, anyway, but some are more elaborate. Usually, the maintenance of an entire road is divided into responsibility by how far down the road your property is, and this makes sense. If your land is a mile down a dead-end gravel road, whereas the first landowner's land is a hundred feet from the paved county road, it wouldn't be fair to have that person pay for anything farther than the portion of the road affected by their coming and going. Regardless, with or without a road-maintenance agreement, some people can or will pay and others won't, and short of a huge cost like a bridge issue, those that want a nice road will usually end up footing the cost and letting it go at that for the sake of keeping peace in the neighborhood. Always find out if there is a current road-maintenance agreement between the seller and the neighbors; usually these and all other agreements between folks are, or should be, recorded at the county and will be disclosed when a title search is done on the property you are buying.

What Factors Are Critical When Choosing Country Property?

Some factors are critical when buying country property that absolutely must not be overlooked! Probably the three most critical factors are the water availability, the sewage disposal, and the availability of electricity. If electricity isn't on the property at the place where you want to build your home, you might be out tens of thousands of dollars or more to bring it in from where it is. Out here, we use a rule of thumb of about five thousand dollars per pole! Phone service might be a huge issue, too, but in this day and age of cell phones, this may be less of a factor IF you get cell service where your country property is! If you are bringing power in, the phone usually goes on the same poles, and the cost is very minimal.

What good is a property that has no water or has no way to dispose of sewage? Most jurisdictions will not even issue a permit to build unless you can prove that the property is suitable for a septic system (sewage) and has a well with a livable amount of water output. In the country, water typically comes from wells in the ground that vary in depth from just twenty or thirty feet to a thousand feet or more. In some areas, such as in valleys that sit over a huge aquifer, you can bet money on how deep the water is and how much is there just by getting information on the wells on the surrounding properties. In other areas, such as in the mountains and hills, you might have one five-acre property with a great thirty-gallon-per-minute well and one next door with three dry six-hundred-foot holes! In these areas, I strongly recommend buying a property with an existing well and also recommend having that well tested for output prior to buying the property, even if there is an existing well log report available. I say this because factors in the ground in some of these areas change, especially over the dry seasons. Also, there is a rare occasion when a well driller inflates the well's output for the owner in order to make the property look better to potential buyers. This is especially true if the landowner is a friend or good client of the well driller. These tests are usually cheap (in the couple-hundred-dollar range) and are well worth it when you are risking everything you own on a piece of property.

If there is no well on the property that you like, your real estate agent can ask that one be drilled prior to the close of escrow and that it have a certain acceptable output, and that the property be tested and approved for a standard leach field and septic system for sewage disposal. The septic approval is usually not overly expensive, and the county health department, which issues the permit, may have enough knowledge about the area that they will issue a permit "over the counter," as they are certain the soils will accept the sewage just fine. In other cases, however, the county will ask that a permit be taken out and that eight-foot holes (or as deep as possible) be dug so they can examine the soils. They may further ask that you have "perk" holes dug, which are small holes a couple of feet deep, at various locations and perhaps at different depths, which are then filled with water and timed as to how long it takes the water to disappear. This determines how the sewage will act when put in the soil. If the soil will not drain, it may not be feasible for a standard septic system, or if it drains too fast, it may have the potential to pollute the groundwater and not be acceptable for that reason. In some areas, an engineer is required to obtain any septic permit at all, and this is more expensive yet.

In the event that a standard septic system is not adequate, there are special "engineered" systems that may work, but those will typically run into the tens of thousands of dollars, as opposed to the three thousand dollars for a typical standard septic system. Some lots are too close to a creek or pond, are too steep, or are too wet, and septic systems are simply not allowed under any circumstance. I bought a nice little one-acre parcel in a tax sale a couple of years ago that has homes all around it on the creek, but since those were built, the county placed a moratorium on allowing septic systems within 150 feet of the creek, and my lot is therefore not buildable unless I negotiate an easement with a neighbor for sewage disposal, which is another story I won't go into! But I only paid a couple thousand for the lot, and you might find yourself spending a hundred thousand or everything you own on a lot, so you can't have such an issue arise.

Now, wells can be a huge problem if one doesn't exist on the property that you have your eye on. You may ask the seller to drill one as part of the deal, but I have almost never seen this happen in my entire real estate career. Wells are expensive, and the seller ordinarily doesn't want to spend several thousand dollars to drill it, nor does he want to take the risk that there is no water in it when he drills it, which may make his property worthless. As incentive, you can offer to raise the price by the cost of the well, especially if the seller seems confident of there being water in the well and boasts about it! Your real estate agent might suggest that you pay to have one drilled, if you have the cash, with the agreement that the seller splits the cost with you or agrees to lower the price substantially if you do get a good well in compensation for you taking such a huge risk. In any case, you do not want to close escrow and own a piece of property that does not have water on it —it is worthless!

How Do I Find the Right Country Property to Buy?

Finding rural property becomes much easier when you have taken the preliminary steps to determine what your intended use is, what factors are priorities, and what factors you do not want for sure, such as poison oak or being too far out for the kids. By this time, you are about ready to make a decision on a specific piece of property and you may have a good feel for the specific areas that are acceptable to you. However, you need to enlist the help of a professional to make sure that you have not overlooked any area that might work for you. A professional can help you narrow down the properties that meet your criteria and financing capabilities.

In fact, the next section on financing could very well precede this chapter, as it is critical in determining which properties you can afford, what type of financing you can expect, and save you scads of time in not pursuing property that cannot be bought under your financing parameters. As an example, if you have a twenty-percent down payment and need a bank loan for the rest, there is no point in looking at some old mobile on your dream property if the owner refuses to finance it, as the bank will not lend on it, and pursuing it is a great example of wasting time chasing your tail! Again, we will go into financing more in the next section, so when I talk about certain financing issues, don't worry that I am getting ahead of myself, as we will be tying all this together soon enough.

When looking for country property, or any property, as far as I am concerned, I am a huge fan of using a Realtor and not just any real estate agent (and this includes your brother-in-law who just got his license—especially not him). To clarify, a Realtor® is a real estate broker who belongs to a professional organization that has established rules of conduct, ethics rules, and has a governing body. A real estate agent is a person licensed by the state you live in to sell real estate, but he or she may not be a "Realtor," who is held to a somewhat higher ethical standard. Here again, there are many licensed real estate brokers who are fully competent and not Realtors, such as most commercial brokers, but for the average home buyer, you should be dealing with a Realtor—and not just any Realtor!

When you are looking for country property, you do not want to settle on just any Realtor. All too often, a buyer, like yourself, calls on some advertisement on Craig's List or in the newspaper and begins to talk to the Realtor who answers the phone or who actually placed the ad in the paper. Now, I have been a Realtor for over thirty years, and you can trust me on this. That Realtor's goal is to "snag" you as a client and develop an immediate bond with you so you would feel guilty talking to someone else. He or she will offer to show you that property and will offer to get a list together for you of all the similar properties in the area, and he or she will certainly make every effort to get your phone number and e-mail to update you daily on every new listing that might fit your needs. All of this is a good thing, and I am sure that Realtor intends to give you his or her best efforts and should be commended for so doing. However, you may be making a huge mistake if you allow this Realtor to represent you at this point. You don't need just any Realtor; you need a highly experienced rural property expert who has extensive knowledge about all the areas around your locale, including neighborhoods, upcoming developments, adverse conditions in the areas, and above all, a working knowledge of how to finance country property. If you have cash, your Realtor needs to know that your cash is like gold on some improved properties and is gold on all bare, unimproved land! He or she needs to understand which properties are not financeable by any lender and know how to negotiate owner financing, especially if your credit is a little iffy or you desire unimproved land and don't have cash.

What you need to understand is that this land purchase is a huge move and will more than likely involve everything you own. If you needed brain surgery, would you want the new intern or his teacher? This decision is almost as important and affects your family's whole life; it should not be left to anyone less than a professional. Select a professional who has at least eight or ten years in the business, and hopefully one who has specialized in rural land and property sales for most of that time. That Realtor may sell in-town residential or even commercial property, as this is where most Realtors' bread is buttered, so to speak, but some enjoy and have much more experience with rural property than others.

Finding this Realtor to represent you doesn't take much time and will make your life so much easier. When you pick up a newspaper or real estate magazine, you will notice that one particular Realtor seems to have mostly country property listings, and a couple might have many listings in the areas that you have identified as potential areas for your purchase. When you drive in the country, and especially the areas that you are intending to purchase in, you will notice one or two particular Realtor's signs on many of the listings. If you then get online and visit that Realtor's website, he or she will probably have some background information about their experience. Every state has licensing information available, which may show when that person was first licensed, but usually the website will suffice. You might identify two or three different Realtors and meet with them or talk to them on the phone. Let them know upfront that you are considering them and a couple of others to represent you in your purchase, but you wanted to meet them first and see if you have a good feeling about them. If they don't understand this, they would be way too immature for my liking. Most will be happy to oblige.

When you do interview them, explain your financing honestly and fully. Let them know of your desires, how much that you have for the down payment, and any credit issues that you have. Let them know what areas you are considering and why. Then ask them if they think they could be successful at helping you buy your desired property. Thank them and let them know that you will talk it over with your wife, dad, or whoever and call them back. See how you feel with each one and meet the one best prospect in person, perhaps when he or she agrees to show you some properties. Most likely, you will like him or her at this point, but on rare occasion, you might have a "turned off" feeling and want to hire someone else. Remember, your priority is your family and your family's needs.

Most property listed with Realtors is listed in one huge database called the MLS (multiple listing service). You as a buyer do not pay the commission or any fee to the Realtor that represents you, the seller does. So all the Realtors have complete access to all the information needed on each other's listings and can show you any of them on the market. New listings come on the market each day, and your Realtor's job is to stay abreast of these so you can see the good deals as they arise. The MLS is set up so your Realtor can have listings that meet certain criteria—such as acreage ranges, price, home size, bare land, or any number of factors—sent directly to you the second it is listed. This is a great feature.

Having said all this, you should also keep your eye on Craig's List (www.craigslist.com), in the local paper, and in the throwdown real estate magazines, and keep your ear open to friends and neighbors who live in the area that you are considering about someone thinking of selling. Many times a person will try to save a commission to the Realtor by selling property themselves, but most property is sold by Realtors sooner or later. I strongly suggest that if you find a piece of property that is a FSBO (pronounced fizbo), which stands for "For Sale By Owner," that you let them know you are more comfortable using a Realtor, and have your Realtor give them a call. These sellers will usually be happy to pay half the commission or so, and the Realtor will usually be happy to settle for this, as if they sell another Realtor's listing in the MLS, that is all they were going to get anyway. If you don't use a Realtor, at least have an attorney look over your title documents and contracts, which is not a bad idea even if you are using a Realtor. We are going to discuss title reports and abstracts of title later, and this is of the utmost importance for rural property buyers, as most of these are much different than those of in-town properties.

Again, your Realtor will probably be great, but if he or she isn't doing their job, fire them and move on. Realtors are just people, and they have the same problems with alcohol, drugs, or psychological issues as any other profession, and sometimes health, marital issues, or some other factor comes into play. You can be nice and compassionate, but it isn't fair to you and your family to allow anything to affect your personal business.

How Do I Finance Country Property and Land?
Why Is It Different Than In-town Property?

I have some great news for you, folks! I am going to explain the ins and outs of financing country property and teach you all of the essential information that you need to know to buy rural land in a way that will be easy to understand, with no complicated concepts, and in a short and sweet way. I will take a little time in the beginning to explain the history of the lending industry, just so you know why buying land and country property is a lot different than buying an in-town house is. Knowing what you are up against when buying rural property will save you an enormous amount of time by not chasing after properties that are virtually impossible to buy due to their price, financing terms, or condition. With this information, you can open the doors to more buying opportunities and get the best deals on property that you can.

I want you to relax and read the following paragraphs casually and not get wound up in trying to memorize anything in them; just grasp the overall essence of the concepts that I present here, which are not anything difficult at all. You will come to see why country property loans are different than in-town residential loans, and the reason that many properties you might want, especially bare land, are challenging or impossible to buy using bank financing.

The first thing you need to realize to understand country property financing issues is that banks must sell nearly all their loans that they make to other investors so they can get more money to lend to the next guy. The banks make their money on the loans by keeping a small part of the monthly payments for collecting the money and sending it on to the investors, which is called "servicing" the loan. The investors that buy these loans are huge mutual funds and insurance companies (institutional investors) with billions of dollars. They purchase massive numbers of mortgages from the banks at one time, and there is no way they could ever evaluate each loan to see if it was a good investment or not. So, up springs FannieMae (short for Federal National Mortgage Association—FNMA), which is really nothing more than an "insurance" company that more or less guarantees that the mortgages being bought by these huge institutional investors will be paid in full and therefore are good investments. Fannie's purpose was to come up with a method to make all these loans meet stringent requirements so they were basically all alike from an investment point of view, and so FannieMae could "insure" these mortgages to the investors so they would feel comfortable buying them in huge blocks and, therefore, help our economy by injecting more funds into it. Prior to Fannie, a bank would lend their money out, and the next borrower would have to wait until someone paid off their loan to get one of their own! You can see how important FannieMae is to our economy. The properties were certified to be in good condition, the borrowers had to meet a certain credit rating, the properties had to appraise at their value by an independent appraiser, and there was nothing out of the ordinary in these huge packages of mortgages. Basically, they were "cookie cutter" properties, made just for the "tract home" buyer, and definitely not for country property buyers, like you, where each property is different and unique! This is the problem that rural property buyers must face. I also want to mention that there are other quasi-governmental bodies, such as "FreddieMac," that function in a similar manner to FannieMae, but you do not need to know or care about any of these. I just wanted to mention this so someone doesn't think that I am ignorant of this irrelevant fact.

Given that nearly all residential loans are FNMA-insured loans, and that country property is anything but cookie cutter, loans are sometimes difficult to get. FannieMae did realize that folks like to live in the country and did stretch their rules to allow for the purchase of homes in the country, but there still are limitations, and Fannie does not ever insure bare land. One parameter that they have, as an example, that affects country home buyers (besides the bare land issue) is that they will not insure large parcels of land, no matter what its value is. I have sold land on forty-acre parcels, and the lender made the loan, but only when we had the property appraised as a smaller residential property that was typical for the neighborhood (five acres, tops, in most cases). This can be tough on you as a buyer because the seller certainly wants to be paid for the additional land, but the lender will not lend on any more than 80 or 90 percent of the value of the home and the five acres it sits on. So the cash requirement to buy the rest is all on you!

If you are buying bare land or a property that Fannie won't touch, all that is left as far as bank financing goes is what is known as "portfolio" loans. This just means that the money belongs to the bankers upstairs with the big, fat stogies hanging out of their mouths and the stockholders of the bank, and they charge dearly for it. They usually only lend it on a short-term basis of five years or less. It is their money, and if you are a rich client of theirs, they will certainly give you more favorable terms than an average Joe. In most cases, they won't even lend to the average Joe. Basically, if you want to buy country property and plan to use bank financing, which most folks do, plan on meeting Fannie's rules or you are screwed. Also, you are dreaming if you think they will lend on bare land. The banks used to do construction loans, but that has all but disappeared due to the economic meltdown of 2007. So, when you are shopping, keep this in mind as well as the following, or you will spend many frustrating weeks, if not months, chasing your tail until you finally come to realize what I have just explained to you here.

So, How Do I Buy Land or Property That the Banks Won't Finance?

So how in the heck do you buy bare land, a large parcel, or a home that needs some repair, some land with a mobile home that isn't on a foundation, or some property like these that doesn't qualify for bank financing? There is always cash, of course, but I have found that most buyers simply don't have bucketloads of it in their bedrooms. Cash is a great tool, and I will discuss in some detail what you need to know about it when buying non-bank financeable property a little later, but for now I want to discuss what I think will be most practical for most of you folks.

There are basically three techniques for buying non-bank financeable properties that come to mind. Two are pretty common, and one is a little less likely but should never be ruled out as a tool for any country property buyer. The first is having the owner act as the bank and "carry" the loan himself. The second, for all practical purposes, is much like the first, and is a lease with an option to buy. The third involves getting a loan from some local private investor who will give you a loan on the property like a bank, except will usually require a much larger down payment and charge a much higher interest rate and will often involve a real estate broker who "arranges" the loan for a not-too-cheap fee. Each one of these financing methods has a place and time when it is the best way to go, and that includes the scary last one! I will fully explain these techniques to you so you will have a full arsenal when you head out to shop for country property.

These financing methods open the door to your ability to find property that you like and allow you to buy property that you wouldn't ordinarily be able to afford. You should also know these techniques because, as much as I hate to say it, many Realtors lack experience in selling non-bank financeable properties and may be inclined to steer you away from these as a matter of convenience to themselves, regardless of how ideal any one of the properties might be for your purposes. Here again, a highly experienced Realtor with scads of experience selling country property can prove to be invaluable, as they will most likely have knowledge of properties and which sellers might lend themselves to these types of financing.

Another good reason to learn a little about these techniques is that if you are a buyer with marginal or no credit history, or you don't have the ten- or twenty-percent down payment, these concepts are critical to you having the ability to buy your own chunk of the earth. If you are short on the down payment funds or have a blemished credit background, you will find that many, if not most,

Realtors will give you a little lecture on how to clean up your credit or suggest that you borrow funds from a friend or family member, or both, and tell you to let them know when you have done so to move ahead with them in searching for property. After all, you are going to be a high-maintenance client, and the amount of work that you will be asking them to do is very often not practical in order for them to make money and support their families. Finding property under these circumstances is a grueling process and frustrating for everyone, and in all fairness, no one can expect another person in business to work for pennies an hour. In all honesty, locating and negotiating property for a buyer with these adverse purchasing abilities takes a huge amount of the Realtor's time that can be spent servicing more well-qualified buyers and leading to many thousands of dollars in commissions.

For those of you who are in this boat, the financing techniques I lay out here are more important than ever! You will have to "take your own bull by the horns" and be prepared to do much of your own leg work in finding and negotiating on a property, but if you are serious about buying your own land or country property, here is your key to success: I have bought and sold more properties than I can count, including before I was a Realtor, using these very techniques. All that it really takes for success is tenacity! You will find yourself literally acting as your own real estate agent and contacting listing agents of properties that you like to learn about them and probe the agent and seller as to their flexibility in financing. I also want to point out that any property might be bought using these techniques that I explain here, including the bank financeable ones. However, most owners who are selling their home will be using the funds from that sale to buy another property and, if it is bank financeable, will prefer to be "cashed out" by your loan from a bank when you buy their property. There are cases where the seller might want to defer taxes on a sale by selling in "installments" or prefer to "carry the loan" because they can expect much more in interest than if you cashed them out. Occasionally, you will run across a hard-headed seller whose property won't appraise for what they want, and they would rather carry the paper for a marginal buyer than lower their price.

At this point, let me give you a huge tip on buying property with these techniques. I mentioned that most sellers are using the funds from the sale of their home to buy another home for themselves to live in. These properties are not good candidates for you folks looking to buy with non-bank financing. The property that you are looking for is what I call "excess" property, or put another way, property where the proceeds will not be needed by the seller to buy another home for themselves or to meet some other cash-requiring purpose, such as to settle an estate with many heirs all salivating over their expected share.

A perfect example of excess property is a piece of bare land that was inherited by some person who lives out of state, has no use for it, and would just as soon get monthly payments rather than a lump sum, as it is money they never expected anyway. Another good example might be property that was purchased twenty years ago by someone who had thought of retiring there, and came to be comfortable with staying in the house or area where they already reside. These folks can opt for cash, but they will have to greatly discount their price on this non-bank finance-able property to get it, and they will very likely end up investing it at a rate that will be far less than what they would receive by carrying the loan. This is a true double whammy to them, and oftentimes, lucky for you, they will have a good country property Realtor who explains this situation to them, and they then prefer to carry the paper than sell outright.

You will find that when you first question a seller or the Realtor who is selling a property for a country seller, that you will be far ahead of the game if you question them as to why they are selling. Make sure you are prepared to "read between the lines," as most properties are listed by new Realtors who have marginal experience and will tell you the seller wants cash, when in reality it is a very poor option for their client. Oftentimes, you or your Realtor can make an offer to the seller and actually get in front of him or her to educate the seller, the Realtor, or both of them on the benefits of what you are offering. You might even try a cover letter with your offer to the seller, especially if the seller is from out of the area. I have had many occasions when an inexperienced real estate agent representing the seller was adamant about my offer not being a good one and was tending to "mother hen" the client by influencing them against my offer when it was obviously an offer that the seller would consider if they were being given sound advice from a Realtor with more experience. Oftentimes, at the chagrin of the inexperienced agent, I have called his or her managing broker and explained my offer and the problem I was having getting it objectively presented. The real estate companies are paid by commissions from the sale of properties, and the managing broker likes to get his or her firm paid. It is far too common that some inexperienced agent is more concerned about portraying themselves to their client as being their "protector" from all evils, including the evil non-conforming buyer, than they are in making real estate deals happen! Brokers are fully aware of this and are often very helpful in bringing some sanity to the table in these cases.

I once made a verbal offer to a Realtor to trade a piece of land that I had that was not buildable, but was a great camping or RV getaway property with a beautiful meadow and creek in a very popular area for part of a down payment on a bare piece of land with a well and septic on it. The "mother hen" Realtor informed me that he didn't think his managing broker would find that property acceptable. I asked him if he would buy it from me for a dollar. He said of course he would. I then explained that what I was asking in value for the trade was a bargain price for such a lot, and that his client might own an RV and agree with me, and I then let him know that I was not there to negotiate with him, or his broker, on this piece of property, as neither of them own any part of it. Now, if I was that property owner's broker, I would have gotten the information on it, including pictures, and contacted other Realtors in that area and found their opinion of value of the land being offered in trade. I might have then told my client what it seemed to be worth and suggested we counteroffer at half of that value in trade, take the rest of the cash, hold firm on the price, and see if we could make it work for my client. It is frustrating when these new real estate agents try to compensate for their lack of knowledge and experience by portraying themselves as all-knowing guardians, but be prepared for it, as I can promise you that you will run into it. I will add that you should do everything you can—in a polite way—to work things out with the seller's Realtor first because you will be burning some bridges when you go over his or her head to their broker, and you may even burn bridges with the sellers, as they may be the Realtor's aunt and uncle! Now, let's get more into the meat of the subject.

One very common way to buy property that cannot be financed by a bank, besides paying cash, is to make the seller an offer with a down payment and ask him to "carry the loan" for you. He becomes the bank, and if you don't pay him, he takes the property back through the legal process of foreclosure, just as the bank would. It is my experience that these owners expect a higher interest rate than what a bank would lend at and also seldom make loans longer than ten or twelve years. All these loan terms are negotiable, and your Realtor can help immensely with this, but you need to take care. I never suggest accepting a loan term for less than about ten years, as in real estate five years is lightning speed, and you will be facing a balloon payment with a still non-financeable property at that time, which can be a real heartache. You can negotiate the price, and you should if you believe that it is too high, but if you believe the price is fair, you may want to stick pretty close to it so the seller is not "turned off" from your offer right off the bat, especially if you have learned that the seller is already reluctant to "carry the paper" (another way we term owner financing) for you.

Speaking of learning about what the seller is "thinking," you need to try and get a sense of what his or her "sensitivities" are when it comes to their feelings on carrying the financing. Let me explain. I have learned over my forty-year career in using owner financing to buy property that each seller has one or two ideas on what is important when it comes to selling their property. Some sellers could not care less about what the down payment is or what the interest rate is as long as they get the price they want. Others are less sensitive to price but want to brag to their relatives about the great interest rate they are getting on the loan that they made. Some, as long as they get a large down payment, are fine with about any interest rate that is proposed and may accept a much lower price. Many folks that carry paper are older and feel it is important that they get paid in full before they kick the bucket!

Regardless, the more that you can learn before making an offer, the better negotiating position you are in and the less chance you will insult or scare off the seller. If you are dealing with the seller in person, you can often find out about some of these feelings just by having a general conversation with them once they have indicated to you that they might consider financing a property for you. For instance, you might say something like, "Do we have any flexibility on the asking price so it's a little more affordable to me?" or "I saw the bank is lending at about three and a half percent right now for house loans, is this about what you were looking at?" or "I'd hate to get caught with my pants down with a balloon payment due before ten years or so and not be able to get financing, any way we could stretch this out ten or twelve years?" and so on. Believe me, you will get an earful, and by the time you get done probing and chatting, you will probably have come to an agreement for the most part that is acceptable to you both. With a Realtor representing the seller, you may just ask him or her these questions outright and then express your same thoughts and feelings and see if you can get them to do a little probing of their client to help the deal along. In some cases, you may just make an offer in writing with all of the factors in your favor and see which factors are apparently of the most importance once you get the counter offer from the seller in writing, or at least some of his feeling relayed to you verbally if your offer is rejected entirely. The Realtor might say something like, "He was fine with the terms but he wouldn't even consider such a price," and you then have good information for your next offer.

When you make an offer for owner financing, make sure you can afford what you are offering. Most importantly, think through the overall costs of getting the property to the point where it fits your needs. So if you can only afford this property's payments if you can live on it immediately, you had better consider all the costs that are going be involved in getting it to that point. If it is an old home that needs a roof immediately and some electrical work, make sure you are prepared to meet these costs and make sure you find out the "worst case" costs for your planning purposes. If it is bare land and you need a well, septic, and power lines brought in, gravel roads built, etc., none of these can be financed and all will take cash—and you had better be prepared to pay them, or you will be making payments on this property and the one you are living in!

If you are offering to pay the entire land off at some point in the future, have a clear picture of exactly how you plan to do this based on reality, or you could lose your entire investment when you get the land taken back by the seller for not paying him as agreed. Sometimes folks like yourself will offer to make payments that are equal over the life of the loan, and when the last one is paid, the land is paid off, which is called a "fully amortized" loan. This is how typical bank loans on houses are. But, many times the buyer will offer to pay just the monthly interest on what is owed to the seller and pay it all off at a later date, or pay big chunks (balloon payments) towards the principal every year or several years with one big balloon payment when the whole loan is due at the end of the loan period. When you are negotiating the terms of owner financing with the seller, always try to get the seller to make the loan "assumable" to any new buyer, so if you do sell, there is already financing in place for the new buyer. Sometimes the sellers are reluctant to allow just any Tom, Dick, or Harry to assume their loan, but you can always include a clause that allows them to "approve" of the new guy. This usually also has a clause in it that is something along the line of "seller's approval cannot be unreasonably withheld," so the seller isn't inclined to try to make the assumable loan non-assumable after all.

This raises another important point, now that we have brought it up. With owner financing, you can negotiate virtually any deal you can imagine, which is not the case at all with bank loans. Let me give you a couple of examples. The seller might be reluctant to sell to you because you are a little shy on the down payment. You might offer to give him a big lump sum in a year because you have an annual trust fund payment coming to you each year. The disbursement is assured, and you can even prove it to the seller if he wants, so he sells to you and you set it up this way. In this case, the seller might have wanted cash, but your annual trust fund payments are big, and he agrees to take that from you every year for five years, which pays the loan off and works for you both!

In another case, the seller might be looking for steady income for five years and doesn't want you running out and getting a bank loan and paying him off; you could agree to a "pre-payment penalty" if you do. Maybe you agree to make monthly "interest only" payments on what you owe, but at the end of each year for thirteen years, pay two thousand dollars towards the principal, and then pay anything remaining that is due at that time. Again, it is whatever you can dream up that works for the two of you!

What you don't want to do is make promises on speculative income that can cause you to not be able to meet your obligations. For instance, up here in Northern California, the pot-growing industry has flourished since the late 1990s, when it was approved for medicinal purposes. Many growers will buy a property with a down payment from their last crop and promise the seller a lump sum each year, thinking that they are going to have plenty of money each year from their gardening efforts. Then, some meth-amphetamine-fueled nocturnal neighbor raids the place in the wee hours of the morning and steals it all, or some hungry gopher, methamphetamine-fueled or not, wipes the medicine from the map, and this balloon payment becomes impossible! Then what? You might be able to renegotiate with the seller, but this would be at his discretion and at his terms, while you are conveniently positioned over a barrel! You should never rely on collecting money that is promised to you from anyone, including money that you are owed from when you sold property, money coming from an inheritance that is still in probate, or a promised gift from a relative, and especially a settlement from a lawsuit. These are all examples of speculative money sources, and if I had a nickel for every lawsuit settlement that was mentioned to me by potential buyers over the years that didn't materialize, I would be in the Bahamas on my private island right now instead of writing this book!

When you do use owner financing, or a lease with an option to buy (which we are about to discuss), always use an attorney or a title and escrow company so you know that you are buying property that the seller actually owns outright and that the IRS, some credit card company, or some other person doesn't already have a lien on. *You absolutely must make sure of this,* and relying on the seller's promise that this is not the case is a mistake of epic proportions! If there is a loan already on the property that you will be assuming, the lawyer or escrow company will need to get a statement from that lender as to exactly what is owed. Many loans are not assumable and must be paid when the property is sold.

From time to time, a seller might want you to make him payments, and he will pay the payments on the already existing loan from the payments that you make to him, which is known as a "wrap around" or "all inclusive" loan. Some sellers feel better doing this because they know those payments are being kept up; if they weren't and that person foreclosed, it could wipe the seller's loan out if he didn't have the money to catch it up in time. The loan that already exists needs to be assumable, even on a lease/option in most cases, or the lender could demand that they be paid in full immediately if they find out about your purchase in this manner.

Another problem that occurs is if the seller takes your monthly payments and doesn't pay the underlying loan. This is illegal in most states, but that isn't much comfort when you lose your land to foreclosure because of it, and all you can do is sue some broke seller who now resides in Mexico! I like to stay away from these situations altogether if at all possible.

Lease/Options

Lease options often come in handy for those folks who have very little cash for a down payment. Oftentimes, a seller wants to sell a piece of excess property, but the market is slow and his property isn't bank financeable, and there isn't a line of buyers at his door throwing money at him. You might find yourself wanting a piece of property but you are low on cash. In these scenarios, a lease with an option to buy could be a great tool for you. A lease with an option to buy is a rental agreement that allows for the person that is renting the property (the lessee) to have the option to buy it at some point. The lessee is not obligated to buy the property, but has the "option" to do so. Oftentimes these agreements will call for a portion of the rent, which sometimes is higher than what other similar properties are renting for, to go towards the down payment, and the purchase price if the renter decides to buy the property later. This is a great tool for the person just getting started out to move towards owning a piece of property by accumulating an acceptable down payment to a property seller.

There are no set rules on these agreements, and much like the owner financing I explained above, you can develop about any terms that you can imagine. I have seen some agreements where the buyer put several thousand dollars up for the option, which was non-refundable, in order to put the deal together. I have also seen a person going through a divorce using the lease option as a means of keeping their name off a property until it was beneficial to do so.

The lease option is typically a two-part agreement. The first part is a standard lease or rental agreement, spelling out the terms much like any rental agreement would, including late payments, pet rules, occupancy terms, and the like. The second part of the agreement is the purchase part, which spells out the terms of the purchase, including how much of the monthly payment is applied to the down payment and purchase price, how much must be accumulated as a down payment before the renter can "exercise" his option to buy, what the purchase price is, what interest rate is to be charged by the seller, and the rest of the terms we talked about in the owner financing section. Some lease options even call for a return of all or part of the option money if the option to purchase isn't exercised; however, most agreements do not. You can always try, though!

There are several benefits to the seller of a lease with an option agreement. First, the seller gets to rent the property and have immediate monthly income; also, someone will be living on the property instead of it being vacant. Vacant homes in the country, where the next neighbor may be far out of sight, can lead to theft and vandalism more often than a rental home in an in-town neighborhood. I have even seen people steal a well pump, along with all the equipment and wire that goes with it! In a lease option agreement, the seller has a tenant who has a vested interest in taking care of the property, instead of trashing it and hitting the road. There is also the high probability that the seller has actually sold his property, especially if the renter is paying a monthly payment substantially higher than what it would rent for—and this is non-refundable. The seller retains ownership of the property, and in most cases can simply evict the renter if he or she fails to pay rent on time or trashes the property.

The tenant does have other rights, though, and these vary from state to state. Here again, spending a few bucks on an attorney to set the agreement up in your favor, and learning what your rights are, is essential. For instance, in some states the courts look at such agreements as actual sales, even though they do not appear as such, and give the tenants much the same rights as a purchaser, including the requirement that they be foreclosed upon to get rid of them (at great expense to the seller) instead of simply evicting them. In any case, you should make sure the seller owns the property and is in a position to sell it, and you should also put "the world on notice" that you have rights by recording a legal document representing your rights under the lease/option agreement in the county in which the property is located. An escrow company and attorney can help you with this, including the title search, to make sure there are no liens on the property. Make sure you read the section here about escrow and title so you have a basic understanding of how to protect yourself in any real estate transaction. Oftentimes, to save money or preserve privacy, the parties will record a "memorandum of an agreement" rather than all the pages of a lease option agreement. This has the effect of protecting your rights, but you should carefully store and protect the underlying agreement that will need to be produced at some point to clear the title of this encumbrance.

Buying Property Using a Local Private Investor's Money

Sometimes you will find a property that you really want, but the seller is not in the position to carry the paper or is simply unwilling to do so, and that property is not a bank-financeable property. Sometimes there is an estate with a bunch of heirs involved, or cash is needed to cover estate taxes. Sometimes the seller is moving out of the state or country, needs a down payment on another property, or has some other issue that makes the seller unable to carry the financing on the property. Now what?

In the real estate world, there is always a group of people who have cash available to invest, which would otherwise not be earning any interest in the bank—banks are "generously" offering one percent interest or less on your deposits! We all know that the stock market is hard to understand, some perceive it as risky, and the monthly payments from it may not be better than the banks'. Many of the folks out there who are sitting on cash are elderly, have bought and sold real estate most of their lives, and many have carried the financing on property they have sold in the past. These folks are comfortable with investing in the real estate market and like the idea of investing their money where it is secured by real estate that they can actually walk out and jump up and down on, which is a little tough in the stock market. They are typically a bit more sophisticated than the average Joe in real estate matters, and they realize that folks like you are out there willing to pay them a much higher interest rate than what they can safely expect by making other investments or keeping their money in the bank.

As an example, right now interest rates are at historical lows. As I mentioned, the investor might get one percent in the bank, and FannieMae insured home loans are running about three and a half percent. At this point in time these investors are asking and getting in the range of five to even fifteen percent on their money, but most often are charging between eight and ten percent. Here again, just like when the owner carries the financing, they become your "bank," and their loan is secured by your property as collateral. They have the same rights to foreclose and take your property away that a bank would have.

So, why would you want to borrow funds at these mafia-type interest rates? Well, you got any better ideas on how to get that dream property you want? Once you find an investor who will commit to your financing, you can almost act like a cash buyer and enjoy the benefits that such buyers have when they negotiate on property (see next section). Oftentimes, the sellers understand that their property is a tough sell for cash and will drastically discount that property in order to get it, and this discount more than offsets the interest rate costs. Think about it: If you buy a property with a loan of $120,000 with a four-percent interest rate, the annual interest is about $4800, or $400 per month. If you get that same property with only an $80,000 loan because you are in a position to give the seller cash on his hard-to-finance property, and the interest rate is double that, 8%, your interest cost is now $6400 per year, or $533 per month. Are you going to forego your dream property for a hundred and thirty three bucks a month? And remember, there are often minimal loan fees, no appraisal fees, and because many private-investor loans are "interest only," where you only pay the monthly interest with the full amount due at some distant period in time (while the bank loan requires monthly repayment of part of the principal, as well as what is called "PMI" in many cases), your payments may even *end up being less*. Just so you know, PMI is a type of "slush fund" that all borrowers with down payments of less than twenty percent pay into as an insurance to the banks and FannieMae that substantially raises your monthly payment while not going to interest or principal! It really kills many a buyer's home affordability. Private loans and owner financing don't have such a burden.

Another thing worth mentioning here is that if the property is in a flood plain, banks will require flood insurance, whereas this is all but unheard of in private financing. If your property is improved with a nice home or mobile, you still may want to purchase flood insurance, but it isn't typically required.

Where do you find the folks with this "private money" to lend? There are basically three main sources. The first is "Uncle Moneybags" or another relative who might be willing to lend you some money. Usually, you can bet on a little better interest rate from family members, but you know how that goes. It gets a little sticky if you get behind on your payments, especially if your family is put in the position of foreclosing on you. For this reason, you or the family member might want to avoid such a relationship, and it is a very good and valid reason to do so. If you do ask a family member, be very organized and businesslike. Have your proposal in writing, the value of the property supported, your repayment plan clearly laid out, and be clear that the proper paperwork securing the loan by the property will be in place and prepared at your expense by an escrow company or attorney, and even a personal note that if you do not pay as agreed, that you actually expect your relative to be businesslike and take your property from you. You will not expect anything less.

Another thing that you might find by getting money from a relative is that they will invest in your property with much less of a down payment on the property than almost every other private investor might require. Typically, the private investors that you approach for a loan will expect at least a third or more down payment from you on the property so that you are very apt to pay them and not just "walk away." This large down payment allows them a buffer from you tearing up the home or improvements prior to them taking it back, protects them against downward fluctuations in the marketplace, and allows them a margin to cover the foreclosure and legal costs if they do have to foreclose on you. As I stated before, most of these "hard money" lenders are elderly and rely on the income from their investments to meet their monthly bills, and it is a rare occasion that they will lend on a property with less than about a third down. I will say that there are folks out there who will do so, but they will check your credit, have the property appraised, and check your underwear before they do! Most private moneylenders expect enough equity where they will simply do a "drive by" appraisal of their own and take a gander at the land you are offering to put up and make a decision on the spot. The larger your down payment, the easier and more likely this decision becomes for them. I will add, too, that a bank loan, with the appraisal and all the other hoops, is usually a thirty-day to sixty-day process, where a private money loan might take a day or two if the lender isn't busy playing golf!

Finding a private lender who is not a family member isn't as hard as you think, once you become aware that they are out there and are looking for you, too. I often see ads in the newspaper where an investor has "money to lend on real estate." As a matter of fact, this is so common that many newspapers have a section for this. The newspapers also might have a section for "money wanted," where you might place an ad for some money. State the terms you might be comfortable with, such as "will pay 8%" or "have $50,000 down on $150,000 property" to entice the lender. You may never meet the lender in person, and I doubt if even one will want you to explain what they are doing! They know exactly what they are doing and will give you a run for your money when you negotiate your interest rate, no matter what percent you put in your ad! Another popular source for these folks is the experienced country property Realtor you are working with. If they have been in the business of selling land and country property for several years, your search for private money won't be their first rodeo. They more than likely have a little black book full of folks who are private money lenders, especially since they can sell a property and get paid if they can get their clients such financing. I have such a book, and I have found myself using the same investors many times.

Another source, one that is more costly but is perhaps the most significant source of private financing, is the real estate broker who acts as a "money broker" for these private money lenders. These folks are licensed to do such loans and abide by pretty strict rules in most states. They typically give disclosures as to the APR (annual percentage rate), among others, and oftentimes the borrower can't get the funds for three days, at which time the borrower has an absolute right to "back out" of the lending agreement. These brokers will have their own black book, and you can bet that many are the same as who answer your ad in the paper, have their own ads in the paper, and are in your Realtor's black book as well. These folks are in this business, and it is competitive, like any other, and they are actively looking for the safest loans with the highest interest rates they can get. These private money brokers network with country property Realtors and are a well-known sources for such money, and they are a valuable resource for both the private investors and the borrowers. Many of these brokers make standard home loans for banks and are good at it. As a matter of fact, most of these loan brokers lend the money of almost any and every bank or savings and loan and will shop for you, and you might get your best rate from them, as opposed to going to "your" bank or any particular lender that only lends its own money.

These private money loan brokers make their money by charging the borrower a percentage of the amount they are borrowing. One percent is known as a "point," which kind of reminds me of a reference to some bookie's "juice," but that is the standard term in the industry. These points are negotiable, but it takes two to tango, and if the broker sticks to his or her guns, you will have to either go elsewhere or accept it. They do deserve to get paid, but there are times that I have seen them ask exorbitant fees.

Oddly enough, here in California, a private lender acting on his own without a loan broker may not make loans for more than ten percent interest or it is called "usury" and is illegal. Making a series of these usurious loans is called "loan sharking," and it is a felony! However, when that same investor uses a licensed real estate broker, there are no limitations on the interest rate and none of these usury laws apply. The philosophy behind this is that the borrower is informed through the required broker disclosures and has a statutory period to opt out of the loan.

I'm Using Bank Financing…What Do I Need to Know?

The first thing that you need to know is that you need a person who is in the business of getting folks like you loans on real estate. This person, just like the real estate agent you choose, MUST be experienced and have at least five or more years working full time in the real estate lending business. Just like real estate agents, the "loan officers," as they are called, come and go through a revolving door. They come in and realize that folks prefer experienced experts when it comes to their money matters and just can't financially or emotionally last long enough in the business to get that experience under their belt. However, just like Realtors, at any one time the majority of warm bodies in the industry are "newbies." Here again, you have to be businesslike and refuse to use your relatives and friends who do not meet the important experience threshold that I am recommending. These folks might be a little "butt-hurt," but you can always promise not to do their dental work until you get the proper experience, and they might get the picture. You can also explain that this property purchase is a major life event and you promised your family that you would do your best job and would use the best folks for the job.

Experienced loan officers will have knowledge of a few things that more inexperienced ones would not. For instance, they will know what parameters that FannieMae now has in order to qualify a property in the country for a loan. These rules change all the time, and have especially done so since the big mortgage meltdown of 2007. Leading up to that period, they waived pest inspections and skirted the borrower's credit issues and income requirements, and this resulted in bad loans on poor-quality properties, which was the perfect recipe for the meltdown. Since that time, the government has tightened the screws at every angle in the lending industry. New rules might have come out yesterday, as this is how dynamic the lending industry is. Also, the experienced loan officer might know of a "loophole" in those rules where they can eke your desired property through when a less-experienced loan officer might not.

Another important reason to use a good loan officer is that they are making many loans. This is important because loan officers are typically paid by a commission on the actual loans that they "close." If you have a car payment, house payment, and the rest of the bills that we all have, you need to make a certain amount of money. These lenders' commissions are based on how many "points" (remember: 1 point = 1% of the loan amount) they charge the borrower. There is no rule on how many points they can charge, and some desperate or greedy loan officers will charge several more than the reputable ones, and the more reputable ones are making many more loans and do not need to "stick it to" their few customers. It is important to know, too, that these loan officers, like car finance people, can make money by selling you a higher interest rate than what you are qualified for, which is a "backdoor" way to enrich themselves at your expense for the entire thirty years of your loan!! A loan officer's reputation in the industry is of the utmost importance. Your experienced Realtor will know a handful of these good lenders because, you have to remember, he gets paid when the deal closes, and if some inexperienced lender screws up his deal from their lack of knowledge or by not being fair with his client, he loses big money, and very possibly a good client!

How about using "your" bank for the loan? Back in the olden days, probably before you were even born, banks valued your business and had a real relationship with you. Nowadays, they like to make you think this is true, but beyond training their minimum-wage tellers to be friendly and use your name, you are pretty much just an account number and a potential profit source. These banks lend from their own money source, for the most part, and are usually not your best lending source. Credit unions are typically owned by their members, and their profit motive is tempered by that fact, so you might find a decent loan at one of these; but make sure you hold off until you have identified who is offering you the best deal.

When you go out shopping for a loan, DO NOT commit to any one lender until you have done your homework and have found your best rate. These lenders, as I mentioned, are paid by commission, and their job is to "hook" you when you come into their office or as soon as possible. Oftentimes, they will be very nice and helpful and then ask for a deposit for the credit report they need to get you a loan prequalification letter. And, by the way, you should have such a letter in your possession when you make an offer on real estate in order to strengthen your bargaining position. Once you pay this small fee, you are somewhat committed, as you sure don't want to drop sixty-five bucks in every loan office you visit! I suggest that you print your own out from a free credit report site (visit annualcreditreport.com, call 1-877-322-8228), and take it with you if you meet a loan officer. If you have a good real estate agent, let that person know of your yearn for fair treatment and a good rate and that you know a little about what you are doing (from reading this book by such a genius!) He might mention this to the lender he is sending you to, and you will find that you are treated very fairly. After all, that loan officer and the Realtor have a relationship based upon their mutual respect for each other's business.

I am not going to go into specific loan details in this book, as that is an entire book all unto its own. I will tell you to discuss with your loan officer the differences between the typical thirty-year loans and shorter-termed ones, like fifteen years, as the rates are much less on the shorter-term periods. Also, you may want to discuss fixed-rate as opposed to variable-rate loans. Far more often than not, I recommend a fixed-rate loan so your risk of ending up with a high interest rate and high payment is gone. But, different loans have a time and a place for their use.

Lastly, when you do talk to your loan officer or your Realtor, make sure you are honest with them about your finances and any other information they might request. These folks are pros and they can best help you if they have a clear and true picture of your life and finances. They have seen all the deaths, inheritances, divorces, and credit problems that you have many times before, and they will best know how to help you with these factors.

What If I Have Cash Moolah?

Well, your financing of country property issues have now become moot. Now, your main goal is to "steal" a piece of property. I say this because everyone I have dealt with who has a huge lump of cash seems to have this thought somewhere in the back of their mind, and I would, too. In the bare land and non-financeable character properties, cash is huge. Almost every seller wants all cash if they can get it, no matter how bad of a tax and financial decision it is to do so. The number of people shopping for property in the country with enough cash to buy the property they are after is few. So we have a high demand and low supply situation, and we all know what that means! In the market for cars, it means higher prices, but in this situation, it means lower prices! We have already learned why money is scarce from banks for land and country property purchases, so we now know that if we have cash to buy with, we have a unique bargaining position with every one of those sellers. If they are represented by a decent country property or land broker, they will know it, too.

Now you need to find a property that will work for you. Even if the property you find is bank financeable, you often can expect a bargain because the seller gets an easy sell without having a bank involved, the borrower's credit history, and such factors, but that bargain won't be anywhere near what you might expect on non-bank financeable property. When you do find a property, you should have already shopped adequately enough to know what a fair price for it is. This is critical, as when you start looking at country property, you will find prices all over the map. Some of these variations will be justified, such as the difference between two five-acre parcels in the same area, but one has a view and the other is in a hole or has junkie neighbors and a poor access road. However, others are just simply out of the ballpark and unrealistic. Having a good grasp on a property's value is essential to getting a good deal with your cash, and you deserve just that, given the supply and demand position you are in. Also, you need to glean as much information as possible about the seller's circumstances as to why they are selling to get a sense of how "motivated" they are. If the seller expresses that he would sell if he can get top dollar and his price is, in fact, high, that is one thing. If, on the other hand, a seller has inherited a ranch in Florida and has to be there to manage the orange harvest without exception in two weeks, and never plans to come back to your state, this seller is "ripe" for the picking! Every seller has factors that are at play when it comes to selling their property, and knowing as much about these thoughts as possible is always beneficial, no matter what method you are using to buy their property.

When you have identified a property and have ascertained its value, which your Realtor can help greatly with, you are prepared to make an offer. With a cash offer, you can close escrow quickly, and some sellers really find this important. Regardless, you don't want to rush escrow where you forego proper investigation of the property with inspections by third parties, such as well experts, or have time to check with the county and neighbors. But you might want to plan on doing these things quicker and make your bargaining position even stronger. Depending on the value of the property, without particular regard to the seller's asking price, you will decide on an offer.

It makes some Realtors and sellers angry and frustrated, but I prefer to start my negotiations when I have cash extremely low. You would be surprised at how attitudes change and expectations drop when some immediate cash is dangled in front of someone's face, and hence why the quick close of escrow is valuable in negotiations. You run the risk of making the seller angry at you when you "lowball" an offer, as well as his Realtor, who has to take the insult to the seller, but usually greed will take over and a motivated seller will at least counter your offer with one that will not scare you away. Many times, to keep from scaring you away, their counteroffer is less than what you or your Realtor ever expected and is a great bargain basement price for the property. At that point, you might come up a little and negotiate further or just grab the deal. The risk of negotiating further comes from the Realtor representing the seller blurting out in the office what a steal somebody is getting on the property, and someone else jumps into the picture, or a relative or neighbor finds out and jumps on it, but here again, do they have the cash like you do? Remember, you can always come up if they don't like your offer; seldom does a "lowball" offer kill a real estate deal because greed is the prevailing motivation in almost every case. And I don't mean greed in a bad way; it is just a word that best and most easily describes each person's quest for the best deal they can get. After all, it isn't like taking candy from the baby or trying to stick you for as much as I can get for this book!

What Are Important Things to Keep in Mind When Negotiating with the Seller?

When you are negotiating to buy property, there is much more to it than the price. As a matter of fact, the price is the easiest and one of the smallest parts of the negotiation process!

When you are negotiating, you are going back and forth with the seller with contracts that will bind both of you to the various terms and obligations once you both sign the same purchase agreement and its related counteroffers. You must protect yourself during this process at all times, like a boxer in the ring, because if you overlook some important issue, such as a needed "contingency" (I'll explain in a minute), you may find yourself losing your deposit or even getting sued! Here again, a good Realtor or attorney is important.

I have covered, and will cover in the following sections, most of what is important when negotiating with the seller, but I wanted to let you in on something I have learned about buying real estate that is true nearly one hundred percent of the time—but not overtly discussed or recognized—and is important for any buyer. Simply stated, real estate sellers' lives change constantly, and as they do, so do their goals and intentions on how they sell their real estate. Sellers develop health problems, family issues, money problems or windfalls, job changes, divorce or marriage, or even just get wild hairs that make them want to travel or experience somewhere else all of a sudden. Sometimes their parents become ill and they must make a move all of a sudden or they decide to go back to school or have children that need to be closer to town. That is a partial list, as any human event or issue can and will arise over time, and each of these will influence the decisions that these folks make concerning all of their life's decisions, and this seems to be especially true of their real estate. I want you to know this because there are times that this can be very beneficial to you in finding and negotiating on real estate.

I have had times when Realtors have told me that their client would sell a piece of property only if they got their full asking price and laughed at the offer that I gave them, only to find out that the wife got a job out of state and ended up telling the husband that if he didn't move, she was leaving him! Needless to say, that was a bargain basement sale! So, when you are shopping, as I mentioned before, tactfully glean as much information as possible from the sellers, neighbors, and Realtors so you know which properties are "ripe" for the picking. If you are shopping and you liked a property, but it was overpriced, keep your eye on it, as people's lives change quicker than you might realize and that property might suddenly appear on the market at a much lower price.

What Is a "Contingency" and Why Are They So Important?

Before we go any further, I want to explain to you what a contingency in a contract is so the rest of our discussion on negotiations and escrows is easy to follow. A contingency is basically a contractual "IF." For instance, if a contract is "contingent" upon the buyer's approval of a well report, septic inspection, or other investigation of the condition of the property (or getting financing or a down payment gift from "Uncle Moneybucks"), the deal is off if the buyer fails to qualify for the loan, get the down payment, or if the buyer finds any report or information that was uncovered in his investigation of the property unacceptable. There should also certainly be a contingency for the buyer to approve the condition of the title that shows all the easements on the property, who owns the mineral rights, liens on the property, and such. Even sellers can have contingencies, such as "contingent upon the seller finding suitable replacement property," but these are more rare. Most real estate contracts have no seller contingencies, and if they "back out" of the deal, they can be sued and forced to sell to you or face damages for not doing so, and this includes when some other buyer comes and offers them a bunch more money after they have agreed to sell to you! In most states, both parties, the buyer and the seller, are entitled to the "benefit of the bargain" that they struck upon the date of the signing of the real estate contract and not the close of escrow later.

Every transaction should have contingencies in it to protect the buyer and allow time, during escrow, to uncover as much as possible about the property. Usually, it is not practical or advisable to investigate a property that you are interested in prior to coming to a contractual agreement with the seller because these inspections take time and money, and without a contract between you and the seller, he may choose to sell to someone else while you are checking his property out. Not having a contingency in a contract and backing out is outright "default," and you may be subject to a lawsuit for any damages caused by you for not upholding your legal obligations in the sales contract. If you backed out of a deal and the next day the real estate market collapsed, and the seller's property lost fifty thousand dollars in value, this could very well be your obligation to pay! Had you had a contingency for inspecting any aspect of the property, you could send a letter within the time you had negotiated as a "contingency period" that you found the property unacceptable; you would be on your way free from any further obligations. The contingency periods are negotiated between you and the seller. As a buyer, you ideally want the contingency period right up until you close escrow, but as a seller, you want the buyer to "waive" his contingencies or his right to have them to disappear as soon as possible. Some in-between time is usually the case, which is fully adequate for a buyer to obtain any inspections or information and have time to consider them.

In some states, the buyer's contingency period continues until he has waived them in writing, no matter what the contract says, and all the seller can do is give the buyer a notice that if the buyer doesn't waive them, he will cancel the deal. If he doesn't give that notice and cancels it, the contingencies remain for the entire time of the escrow. In other states, when the time expires as negotiated in the sales contract, the buyer has been "deemed" to have approved all items unless he or she has actually objected in writing to those matters prior to this expiration date. It is very important to actually investigate all aspects of the property and get your inspections done in any case, as when you close escrow, you have very little recourse without spending huge money on legal fees!

A partial list of typical inspection and other contingencies are:

- Well quantity and quality
- Septic inspection
- Pest inspection for termites, dry rot
- Roof inspection
- Whole house inspection by a licensed home inspector
- Your approval of the property corners and boundaries
- Your right to investigate the property as to any other aspect that you desire
- Your ability to qualify for and obtain financing
- Your approval of the written disclosures either required of or requested from the seller
- Other inspections that make you feel comfortable

I will cover the well and septic issues in more depth later, as they are so important (MAKE SURE YOU READ THEM!), as well as a bit about the property lines and corners, but I want to just briefly touch on a couple of the above items here before we move along.

The pest inspection is done by a licensed "Pest Control Operator" whose rear end is on the line if he misses anything that he should have found in his inspection. Dry rot, termites, wood-destroying beetles, and other pests can cause tens of thousands of dollars in damage to a home. The pest inspector, which is loosely called a "termite inspector," uses a probe and stabs around in the attic, the crawl space under the home, on the decks, and in any other "accessible area" of the structure being inspected. The word "accessible" is a key term. If the inspector cannot access a portion of the property, he will note that fact on his report and move along. Such areas might be where he is too large to crawl under the house, as it was not constructed high enough off the ground (a breeding ground for pest problems), or it could be a place where the seller has piled personal property or debris. These areas are suspect and should be inspected once the items are removed to allow access. I say this because I have had a bad experience with a crooked Realtor who used this method as a routine way to commit fraud on unsuspecting buyers. I have seen him instruct a seller to pile plywood and construction materials in front of areas that had obvious problems to the siding and probably even in the wall structure, so this area would be noted as "not accessible"! His other trick was to replace wood siding over a wall that was termite eaten or rotten to the point that all that was holding the roof up was the siding. He made a lot of money buying "fixer uppers" and covering up twenty thousand dollars in damage with two hundred dollars of siding! So you might keep your eye out for such newly worked-on areas of the structure, and if you are suspicious, you can even pay to tear it open to have it inspected. Your Realtor will know all about this, or had better, if they are worth their weight in you know what.

As far as the roof inspection goes, use a licensed roofing contractor and make sure you choose the inspectors that you use for all inspections so they have some loyalty to your interests, instead of watching out for the seller. Most are straight up, but you certainly should not assume that this is the case. After all, if I own a hundred houses and use various roofers in the area, and you are the new person on the block with your one home, who "butters" the roofer's bread the most?

A relatively new industry that has sprung up in the last twenty years is the "whole house inspector." These folks have taken steps in many areas to establish a code of ethics and a professional status. They check things like electrical, plumbing, appliances, heaters, and thermostat operation, look for code violations, and much more, and then issue a report on what they have found. Typically, their contracts limit their liability if they miss some item to the two hundred bucks or whatever you paid for the inspection, but more than likely you would have missed that and a bunch more had you not hired them. It is hard to go wrong using one of these folks to inspect a property for you, and I have personally never had a bad experience with one of them, as long as you keep in mind that there are always some things wrong with 100% of homes and you don't get too carried away over the small stuff.

Now, as far as "disclosures" go, in many states the seller of a home is required to fill out a seller's disclosure statement that informs the buyer, to the best of the seller's knowledge, of any defects in the property or problems with boundaries, noise or nuisances in the neighborhood, and many other such items. The seller is putting his rear on the line when he does this, as this could be grounds later for you to claim that you were lied to in order to be induced into buying property at a certain price that you otherwise would not have, if you had known of these "material facts." Sellers are strongly advised by their Realtors and attorneys to come clean and be honest for their own protection when filling out such disclosures, and most of them are, but there is always that ten percent—hence, inspectors and your diligent inspections! As I stated, many states require such disclosures, but if your state doesn't, that does not mean that you can't find one on the Internet or from your real estate agent and ask that it be completed as part of the deal. Just be aware that some states have the underlying legal philosophy that a property's condition is entirely the buyer's problem to contend with, that all sales are "as-is," and that the "buyer beware" statement is of the utmost importance to heed. Other states, on the other hand, afford the buyer much more legal protection by realizing that a sale can only be valid, even if it is an "as-is" sale, when the buyer is actually informed of exactly what "as-is" means, and this is what the mandatory seller disclosure statements are all about.

As far as bare land goes, there is a trend that is moving towards inclusion of a disclosure statement for those sales, but it has not quite become law in most states and may never do so. Just so you know, disclosure requirements on over four units, such as apartments, and commercial properties are not typical, either, because the law figures that if you are a big enough boy or girl to jump into these businesses, you are big enough to check them out yourself!

As far as the last one in the list, having to do with "any other inspections," I have had clients pay for a cat urine inspection and had others have the property examined for chemical residues, as they heard it was used as a crank lab by prior owners! You might have inspections as well if there is spilled oil or odd odors on the property, or anything that you don't like or are uncomfortable with. It never hurts to be overly cautious.

What the Heck is "Escrow"?

Escrow. Hmmm, you have heard it mentioned many times, but you are still wondering exactly what it is. You hear statements like "we are going to escrow" and "when we open escrow" and "while we are in escrow" and "close of escrow" all the time, and it almost sounds like it is a place or some tangible thing that you can hold in your hands. In reality, escrow is nothing more than a time period.

This period starts when you sign a contract with the seller and ends when you and the seller have done everything you agreed to and the ownership of the property actually passes into your name by a deed to you from the seller and upon the recording of the deed at the county recorder's office where the property is located, if that is part of your agreement, which it always should be.

During this "escrow period," all the things that you and the seller agreed to must take place, and usually there is an independent person who oversees that all these things are done as agreed, and who, in the end, gets instructions from both parties to go ahead and transfer ownership, as they are satisfied with the other person's actions. During escrow, the buyer gets his loan in place and makes all his inspections and investigations that he or she wanted and has checked out the title to the property and found that it was acceptable, and the seller has fixed what he was asked to fix or replace. The documents, including loan documents from the bank or the seller, are prepared and signed, and the deeds are prepared to transfer ownership or represent the buyer's interest in the property. Basically, all the terms of the purchase agreement between the buyer and seller are satisfied in full, and lastly, the escrow holder is instructed to "close" the deal and make everything legally final.

I will share with you, just so you know, that the documents used to sell property vary from state to state, as do the escrow and title procedures. In California, we use "deeds of trust," primarily to evidence debt, while in some states "contracts of sale" are common, where the deed and land ownership remain in the name of the seller. Some states typically use "mortgages," which have different characteristics than both of the above, but they are all "debt instruments" and often all referred to as mortgages. Many times, these different methods to secure debt are used in each state due to their unique benefits to the lenders. For instance, many golf courses in California are sold under "contracts of sale" because those contracts allow the lender to come right in, if so written, and take control of the golf course if it is being ruined, even though the payments are current, while a deed of trust that is used on almost 100% of most home and land sales in California would require many months for the lender to get on the property, and the lender's entire security would be ruined! This isn't something that you should be overly concerned about, but be aware of what is being used in your area and whether it is typical, and examine what your rights are under whatever debt instrument is being used in your case.

Also, in some states, there are companies that handle title and escrows that are very reputable and inexpensive, such as here in California. In some states, the Realtor handles the escrow and an attorney examines the title and puts together a report on what is shown from the county records as being against the title. I personally do not agree with a Realtor having that capacity, and if there is some other alternative, I would use it, such as having an attorney do it that is paid by both parties to be independent. The real estate broker may have a big commission coming if the deal closes and may overlook one party or the other's rights or obligations. He may also favor his long-time client over some new person to the area. As far as the lawyer doing the title search, I would want to read any agreement that he has, in case he misses something, and I would hope that he had a good reputation and some insurance for his malpractice or incompetence! As far as I am concerned, any state not having title and escrow companies, which are usually in one building and operate as one entity, as we have here in California, needs to get with the times!

What Important Things Should I Include in My Contract with the Seller?

When you are negotiating with the seller on country property, you will be covering, among other things:

- How long and where the escrow is to be
- What inspections the buyer wants and his rights to cancel the deal based upon them
- Who pays for what inspections, title costs, escrow fees, and other costs
- How long the buyer has to approve the condition of the title and other contingencies
- The terms of any seller financing
- What personal property goes with the sale (appliances, livestock equipment, tools, etc.)

- When the seller has to move and when the buyer can move in
- What things the seller has to repair or replace during escrow
- How the property corners are to be marked or surveyed (see the section on this)

I have covered much of these items in the previous discussions, but I will briefly run through some other thoughts on these matters that might come in handy for you.

As I stated, your escrow period should be adequate to allow you to get the financing from a bank, if you are using one, and satisfy all of your contingencies as to the property's condition. It should also be an adequate time for the seller to move from the property if you are planning to move into it, or vacate it if you plan to rent it. There are times when the seller will want to stay a while after close of escrow so they can find a place to buy once they get the money from the sale of their place, or they can't close escrow on the place they have already bought until they get paid for the property you are buying from them. This situation comes with some inherent problems. For instance, what if the seller stays longer than planned, or during his move out he backs the U-haul truck into the side of the house, or he lets his relatives move in and they refuse to leave when asked? Often, you will have the escrow holder keep a substantial portion of the seller's funds in escrow with an agreement that a certain amount will be given to the buyer for each day that the seller remains in the property, and for any damages caused to the property by the seller after close of escrow. In turn, sometimes the buyer needs to move in before escrow closes, and usually a standard rental agreement is created for the protection of the seller, including an appropriate deposit from the buyer.

Make sure you are careful to include any personal property that is on the property that you expect or desire to be included in the sale. Some typical items might be woodstove inserts, freestanding appliances, water tanks and livestock equipment, such as cattle squeezes, portable horse panel fencing, as well as any plants that might be in pots that can be removed. If there are vehicles or tractors involved, these items should have the titles delivered to the escrow holder and the appropriate transfer documents should be prepared. I recommend that you or your Realtor make a list to be given to the seller in the negotiations and included as an addendum to the contract, clarifying the property to be left and including items that, even though they are considered "included real property" in the eyes of the law, can be removed and taken by some perverse justification. This might include exterior horse arena lighting, gates, plants in the ground, irrigation equipment, and such items. Look over the property and include anything in the contract that you might want and is necessary for the care, improvement, or maintenance of the property, such as riding mowers, spray equipment, or fencing materials you might want that are lying unused around the property. Make sure you include everything, even if the seller clearly states "oh, you can have that, I have no use for it where I am going," as when he moves, his nephew that is there helping him move will have a use for it!

I also want to mention something that comes up occasionally in country property sales. Sometimes the seller has adjoining property that he is selling. When you negotiate your deal on the property you are buying, you might ask for a "first right of refusal" on that property, so if he sells it later, and you find the price to be right or great, you have the right to buy it over the person that he has agreed to sell it to, and at the same terms. You might also consider a lease option on the property or some other way to "tie" it up for your use and purchase it at a later date. Your purchasing the one you are buying gives you leverage now that you will not have at a later date. Also, if you would find that it would be of value to obtain a right of way "easement" so you can access the property you are buying through the seller's other property, such as because of a ravine, waterway, or some other factor, including future developing or subdividing, include this into the negotiations for sure or you will pay dearly later.

Are There Any Other Critical Legal Issues for Me to Worry About?

The short answer is YES! I will tell you some of the major legal concerns that I have when I buy country property that are concerns that every one of you should have as well. Again, I am not a lawyer, and it is certainly not my intent to give you legal advice here, but I'd like to inform you about some stuff that you should at least be aware of when you buy country property, or any property, for that matter.

When you have a lawyer or title company look at the title for you, they do just that and not much more, in most cases. They report to you on things that are known and are evidenced by the county records that have been "recorded" in the county recorder's office. The purpose of "recording" deeds, lease options, land contracts of sale, and such things is to make the entire world aware of someone's rights in a property. In the real estate world, everyone is bound with the responsibility to check these records for what is in them prior to buying, lending money on, or making any other decision concerning a particular piece of property. If you buy or lease/option, or lend money on a property, and you didn't check the title and there is already a loan or it doesn't belong to the person you bought it from, this becomes your problem for not doing so. The person who has clearly recorded their rights and interest in a property before you did has the full protection of the law in almost every case. This is why you always record things at the county, so your rights are protected from someone borrowing against or selling property that you have rights upon. If this happens, your only rights are against the person that "scammed" you and not against the rightful owner of the property. Here again, you'll see the importance of a lawyer.

BUT—and a huge but—you can run into problems with the

property's title even if the title search comes up clean. The law usually requires you as a real estate buyer to act businesslike and prudently by inspecting and investigating the property thoroughly yourself by visiting it and looking for others that may have rights upon it that are not of record. If you do not make this effort and someone claims rights that could have easily been discovered if you did, you are generally bound by the rights of those folks no matter whether or not they recorded their rights at the county! Let me give you some examples of what kind of issues you run into like this, especially on country property.

First, one of the most common occurrences of such a situation is where the neighbor is using a road that goes across the property you are buying. They may have been using it for years to access their property or just because it is a shortcut to their mother's house down the road or to the fishing hole. If they have been using it for a certain period of time, which varies from state to state, they actually could have permanent rights to do so, which is known as a "prescriptive easement." When you visit the property for your required "diligent" inspection and investigation, you might see tire tracks, a gate to the neighbor's, or some other "red flag" that should tip you off. Now, you are under a duty to investigate this situation prior to purchasing the property during the contingency period. You would then ask the neighbor, point blank and directly, if they had rights, and let them know you might allow them to use it with your permission to be neighborly. At least have a friend with you who could testify to their answer if this ever becomes an issue, but the most proper and legal thing to do is for you to get their rights or the fact that they have none in the property in writing, which is known as an "estoppels" document. Your Realtor should be happy to help you with this so you don't cancel the deal and his or her commissions! Another situation might come when you see evidence that someone is grazing their cows or other livestock on the property. It's good to check that out, too, as well as anything else you see that you "wonder" about.

Also, even if your title report shows that you have a legal right of way (easement for ingress and egress) to a property you are buying, and you go to the property and the gate to it is locked or the road is blocked with cars, boulders, fencing, logs, or anything, this is a huge red flag! Not only can someone take rights to your property by using it for a certain number of years, they can take your rights away by denying you use of them for that same number of years! Time to sic the Realtor on them! And make sure you never take the Realtor's word that it is all "straightened out," as folks tend to learn their rights when things like this arise and raise them later and deny ever speaking to you or your Realtor. Again, the estoppels document is the important fix for these types of matters and should be used!

It never hurts to talk to a neighbor about the boundaries of the property for the same reason. Hopefully, the property corners are marked (because you required the seller to do it in escrow), and you can see if any fences are not in the right place. The neighbor may be claiming right to use that property on his side of the fence or may even claim that he had been using it and paying taxes on it and now "owns" it, no matter what the deed description says. This is known as "adverse possession," and while unusual, it is far from unheard of when you are out in the country. Some folks, when buying a large parcel out in the country, will still buy it and just get an agreement with the neighbor to pay the costs to survey it and straighten it out with the county. A fence that is fifty feet in the wrong place on a twenty-acre parcel of mountains might not be worth thinking about, but this should be handled by a lawyer and hopefully in escrow and by the seller at his cost.

Another thing to watch out for is when you buy a property and the seller's sister or someone else is living on the property, and the seller tells you as part of the deal that you get to deal with the "tenant." You figure you will just throw them out after you buy it, and you don't ask them about what they are doing there. Then you close escrow and go to evict the tenant, and they claim that their dead uncle, who used to own the property, told them they could live there until they die! And worse yet, everyone in the neighborhood was aware of this. Now you have inherited a tenant who is living in your house and is paying no rent for the rest of his or her life! Here again, the law expects you to be a "grown up" in business and diligently investigate any such potential rights. Here, the key word is "diligent," or that amount of effort that any reasonable business person would use. I am sure the rights of such folks vary from state to state, but the adverse possession and prescriptive rights are based in old common law from when we were a colony of England, and like many of those laws, were based upon "equity" to all involved. This can happen in country property, but is not any more uncommon in rental properties in town!

What About Surveys and Finding the Property Corners and Boundaries?

"Dang, I knew you were going to bring this up!" This is probably what a typical country property seller is thinking when you bring it up. You would think that everyone knows their corners and that all land is surveyed, marked, and that the legal description in the deed is clear and exact. In modern times when land is subdivided into smaller parcels, this is sometimes true, depending how "backwoods" the state you live in is. However, up until the 1960s in California, and currently in some states, property was just "created by deed." This means they would just create a deed describing the property to be sold, such as "the west twenty acres of the north half of the south quarter of my property, known as the 'Broke Gold Miners' Mining Claim," and that was it. Back in the eastern states that were the original thirteen colonies of the United States, and in some surrounding states such as in Ohio, they would describe a property as "beginning at a large locust tree out by the river near where the creek runs in and off in a northerly direction through a white birch grove about 1325 feet to a boulder lodged in the side bank of an old creek bed about halfway to the top," or some similar way. Corners were seldom set, and if they were, they were often in the wrong place. Even if the person who set them did a good job and used known government survey monuments that were set over a hundred years ago, as many were, many boundaries were still off, as the surveyors that set those government monuments had very little oversight and most really enjoyed their whisky as they worked!

Often, country properties are fenced, and the boundaries are acceptably marked for most folks, and the neighbors and the seller have always just lived with where they are. Occasionally, some adjoining neighbor had a survey that "jives" with what everybody is thinking. Sometimes the land you are buying has actually been surveyed. Sometimes this is a problem, as surveys are costly, and many sellers refuse to pay for them. So, you are in a grey area that will push your comfort level. Most of the time I have found that if the seller marks them for me or I talk to the neighbors or hike around, I will find old fences or some other indication of where the property is to the point that I can accept what I have. Usually, this problem is only bad on huge parcels of 160 acres or more, when land parcels were all huge, because as they became smaller, more attention was paid by all the parties to be accurate and more clearly mark the property. You can always ask the seller to pay a surveyor to mark the property lines or even require a survey, and you can offer to pay all or part of the cost if this is important to you. I just wanted you to be aware of what you are going to run into as far as the property lines are concerned, so you don't say I left something important out!

So now you have found your piece of earth, and I have given you some good information to allow you to negotiate, finance, and protect yourself when buying rural property. Now you need to make it usable, livable, and save money and time as you do. The following section is all about that part of the process, and it is a fun read that you will find very valuable as you bite into developing it.

Section II

How to Develop

Country Property

Section II — How to Develop Country Property

Okay, I Got the Property—Now How Do I Develop It Best (And Save Bundles of Money)?

All right, folks, we made it to this point using my thirty-someodd years as a real estate broker. Now, we are going to use my forty years of experience of actually developing both bare land and property with homes on them. When I started, I was young and dumb and full of energy. I jumped into developing my properties with both feet while I was enjoying the bliss of ignorance. I have made every mistake imaginable, including everything from tipping a backhoe over, stepping on more nails than I can count, and falling a huge tree on my pickup, just to name a few incidents. To this day, every time I go to do something, I see that look of a mixture of distrust, disdain, disgust, disappointment, disrespect, and a bunch of other "disses" in my wife's eye as she readies the medical emergency and fire department numbers for my project! And, as always, I just brush it off and shake my head in disbelief that she still has such feelings right up until they are loading me in the ambulance or putting out the fire!

I will talk mostly about developing bare, unimproved land, but much of what applies to bare land is fully applicable to further developing or changing a piece of property that already has a house, barn, roads, and other improvements. I will just throw in some useful thoughts from time to time concerning these already-developed properties, and those of you who are more concerned with starting with bare land should take heed of those as well, because when you get done, you will have that kind of improved property to deal with!

Start with a Good Site Plan

It may seem like an unnecessary step, but it is extremely helpful to either draw, or have drawn, a good site plan that is a to-scale representation of your property, including contour lines showing the elevation changes. I have a contractor, whose dad was a surveyor, who helps me out, and some folks use a draftsman or engineering firm that has a lower-priced trainee they can rent. The elevation information is usually already available and can be transposed onto a "parcel map" that you can usually get from the county. If the property has been surveyed and there is a survey map available, these maps are much more detailed and accurate than a parcel map, and you will be ahead of the game. When you do make your site plan, make it as accurate as possible so hard-to-find underground features can be located by measuring from some prominent point, such as a marked property corner or corner of an existing building, so the site plan is as useful as possible when you need it.

To begin with, a good site plan will consist of a drawing that shows the following:

- The property lines
- Any easements across the property
- Any creeks, ponds, drainage swales, or ditches
- Any power lines, gas lines, waterlines, or other utilities that might exist
- Existing drives, culverts, walkways
- Existing buildings, barns, sheds, pens, corrals, fencing, etc.
- Any large trees, boulders, or other physical features to save or work around
- All areas over 30% in steepness (as these are usually un-buildable)
- Building setback areas required from creeks, roads, wells, property lines, or other features
- Your existing or proposed well and its setback for sewage disposal, as required
- Your existing or proposed septic tank and leach field (and proposed replacement field) location
- Any proposed roads, building sites, livestock areas, or-chards, gardens, barns, etc.
- A "north" marker showing the site plan's orientation
- The neighbor's well, septic, and other features that can af-

fect your property's development

- Any archeological, environmental, historical, natural, or other significant features of note

With this plan, you can plan and communicate your ideas and requests with your tractor drivers and other workers, as well as with your family. You will also need a site plan with some of this information on it in order to obtain many types of permits from the county that you live in that are required to develop your property, such as the septic permit, well permit, and building permits. If the property already has a home and some other improvements on it, you can avoid digging or plowing through underground waterlines and electrical lines, as well as more mundane things like planting a weeping willow tree over your septic leach lines that will soon lead to them becoming clogged and needing to be replaced at great expense. You should always ask the seller of property that you are buying to show you the waterlines for faucets, irrigation, the leach field area, and any other such underground improvements, or anything that would be important to know for drawing your site plan, as mentioned in the above list. You will be surprised at how helpful such a site plan is and how much money it saves you in the long run. One good example is that if your septic tank needs to be pumped or your leach lines need to be replaced, you can spend a hundred bucks or more to locate those for the work you need, while with your accurate site plan and a tape measure, you can go right to it.

This will be a huge selling feature when you go to sell your home, as many sellers will not have this to show any prospective buyer!

Get to Know the Property Like an Old Friend

When you first buy property, head out to it for several days and spend all day and even all night on it if you can and get to know it. You will be surprised at all the things you learn about a piece of property by experiencing it throughout the day and night. Now a small flat piece of property will not take as much time to get to know as a large piece, but it still should be "friended," to use a Facebook term. On the larger, woodsy, rocky, hilly pieces, you will hike and explore, and I can promise you that you will learn things that will awe you in small ways, if not in huge ways. You might find that one knoll that overlooks a meadow or distant mountain range you never even knew was there. Or you might find that spot that has the perfect exposure for all-day sun without the need to remove majestic trees, unlike the other building site you had in mind. You might find a rock outcropping that is so unique that ninety percent of the perfect rock garden you have always wanted is already built by nature, or a spot on the creek where a waterfall is in view. You may find on your smaller parcel that at five o'clock in the morning, the neighbor's thirteen fighting roosters start crowing, or his dogs like to bark all night! There is no telling what you will find, including another spot to place your home, but I know that I have spent hundreds and hundreds of hours on some of the properties that I have owned in the California foothills, and built my home and then found things a year later that I had missed. Any way you look at it, this time you spend on the land gives you an intimacy and relationship with it that you can get no other way. You may very well find a place to put your home or a place to build a road to some meditation spot that hugely increases your property's value. Spending this time is time well spent, and I cannot recommend it enough before you make any moves on developing your property.

Another huge benefit of spending time on the property is that you will come to know its terrain for building roads, walking trails, and perhaps where best to clear brush and trees for fire protection or some other such purpose. After all, if you have a huge open meadow amidst some thick woods and you are looking to clear for fire protection purposes, then that meadow has all the work done for you! Every property that you develop for a house, barns, gardens, or any purpose will have a drainage issue for the water when it rains or for the snowmelt. Knowing your property helps with things such as this, as well, but without explanation, finding that one best site for your home is usually the most valuable reason to learn your property.

Practical and Money-Saving Considerations
When Developing Property

When you go to develop your land in the country or further

improve the ranchette you bought, you will want to temper your ideas and thoughts with a little dose of financial reality. You will also want to include some other practical considerations from a standpoint of actually making the best use of your property in an efficient way. Just because you found some "Garden of Eden" area nestled deep into your property when you were out becoming "one with the land" doesn't mean that you should immediately put this site in "concrete" for your home site. There are many more considerations that you must take into account before such a decision is made, unless you have actually run across a money tree on the property!

The first thing you need to know is that running waterlines from the well to your home site, barns, and other places, as well as electricity and other improvements, costs money. If you have power lines right on the border of your property and you build within a couple hundred feet of that pole, your power costs might run around three thousand dollars to set your meter box at and hook the power to it. On the other hand, back in the "Garden of Eden" area that is a thousand feet back into the property, that power cost might be about three poles away plus the three thousand we talked about, or a total of around twenty thousand dollars. Then, you have to build a drive to it, with a bulldozer possibly, as well as haul in many loads of gravel at three hundred bucks a load to get to it, and put culverts under the road in a couple of locations that can run a thousand buck or more, depending on how much water they have to carry through them. I am not saying to not do this, I am just saying to get your costs clear and make sure they fit your budget before you do. You will also want to make sure that the area that you have chosen to build is suitable for a sewage disposal system. Often, one area of a particular property is fine, whereas others are not for one reason or the other. Also, if you are planning to be gone driving the country in your motor home all summer every year, you may want your home within view of a neighbor for security purposes.

Can You Help Me Actually Develop the Property and Give Me Some Great Tips?

You are talking to the right guy! I have developed nearly a hundred parcels of country land in my day and have learned some good lessons. With just a few tips, your experience will be much easier, trouble free, inexpensive, and your property will be a showplace to be proud of. I was going to put this next section of the book later, but it is so important of a concept that I want to include it now, and I even coined the word "macroscaping" for it. Even my spell checker doesn't like it!

Macroscaping—The Art of Painting a Picture On Your Land Using Its Natural Features!

I call this the art of "painting a picture upon the earth, using a bulldozer, a backhoe tractor, and a chainsaw as my brushes!"

I wanted to explain this concept now, so as we talk about other development factors, this important one does not get overlooked in the hustle and bustle. Let me explain. When you bring in a bulldozer or tractor, crews to clear the trees and brush off your property, or at any juncture where an opportunity arises to capitalize on some physical feature of your property, you do not want to miss it. A good such example is when I once had a tractor driver up on a knoll clearing a site for my home and cutting into the hill with a bulldozer. I was working and I had to leave all day when he was tearing into the ground. I was using this person for the first time; he was from a local construction company that was a major road builder in the area, including some of our major freeways. His boss was a nice guy, and it was a very professional and well-managed company. However, he was not familiar with the aesthetic aspects of developing country property, like another bulldozer driver (AKA "cat driver") that I used, and I made a huge mistake by not being there. As this cat driver gouged his way into the hillside, he uncovered twenty huge boulders, some nearly as big as a Volkswagen! These boulders can be used to dramatically enhance your building site in many ways. I have used them as borders on building pads on the sides of hills where I filled in against them and made awesome terraces that appeared as natural features, and you couldn't pay to have the boulders brought in to do such a thing. I have used them to enclose a portion of my yard so it became a private prehistoric setting, unlike any property I have seen. Anyway, I came up to the property after work and this cat driver had pushed every one of them off a steep hill and "out of the way." My heart sank, as there was no way to feasibly recover them, and my chance to turn my property into a magnificent showpiece at almost no cost was lost forever!

Rather than try to explain how to "macroscape," it is best that I give you examples of what I have done so that you can grasp the general concept of what it consists of, as there is no one way to macroscape.

This is one good example of what "macroscaping" is all about. On one particular property, I had various areas that were dominated by different types of huge oak trees for about a hundred-yard stretch as you drove up my driveway to my building site. One variety was primarily black oaks, another was mostly a valley oak type treed area, while the two others were scrub oaks and live oaks, but all were grown together in one heavily forested area and had a few strays of the other types of trees scattered within their unique niches, with thick blackberries under them. No one would have noticed these four distinct "mini-forests," but when I was up spending time learning about and enjoying my land, I happened to spot this while I was sitting at a distance on a rock drinking the last half of a twelve-pack of Sierra Nevada Pale Ale! When the "cat" was on site, I had the cat driver clean out underneath these trees and carefully remove the straggler trees in each grove and had him take a few out between the different varieties to further expose their unique differences and visually define the individual groves from each other. I brought in some boulders and dug down in the ground a little and had them placed and half buried, as though they had always been there, and I used a chainsaw and exposed the mossy seasonal creek that had been buried in the berry vines and brush that ran through the area, having been careful not to let the tractor driver touch it with his machine, which would have made it completely unsalvageable as a natural feature. It turned out so very magnificent, and every person that visited me had to drive through it to reach my house, and most would want to walk back to it to take it in further!

One twenty-acre property that I bought had the most stunning view down a huge canyon to its mouth, where it met the Sacramento Valley. I bought it just for that reason. But, as I came to learn from my time spent there, just below the view there was a huge spring that ran across the ground. It caused a huge green patch of grasses and bog-type growth that was fed by a spring near my property line and uphill from my building site. Just beyond that boggy area, buried in the poison oak and scrub brush, was an old rock wall from days past, supposedly built by either the Portuguese or the Chinese, depending on whom you asked. It ran for the full length of my property. When the cat came in, I "captured" all the spring water into a basin at the top of the property near where the spring was coming from the ground and built a small holding pond there, where I installed a funnel with a garden hose clamped to it. This gave me irrigation water for my home site and a shower on my property, which had no well at that point. I had the cat go down to the end of the bog area and dig about a quarter acre pond that was about ten feet deep. I used a chainsaw and the cat and exposed the rock wall for the full length behind the pond, as a backdrop to it. I put some huge boulders in some strategic locations and removed some big trees to further enhance the canyon view. I cut all the lower branches from the trees to make them appear neat and upright, thinned them out, and removed all the leaning and unhealthy trees and branches. Now, from the building site, you looked over this beautiful natural-looking pond, framed by the rock wall, and down the canyon, which resembled a smaller grand canyon with a fully unobstructed view! I doubled the value of the property almost overnight!

On yet another property on flat farm ground, I built a two-acre lake with two islands and buried it in weeping willow trees and redwood trees with huge boulders that I actually brought in from the hills. It was a legend in the area, as these farmers could not grasp some guy coming in and taking up good almond tree ground with a fish pond!

On other properties, I have used gold mining cobblestones to construct massive fire pits and rock walls that were almost identical to the old Chinese ones. I have rappelled down cliffs to fall trees from them to expose a view that only I knew was there, and have used the natural lay of the land and materials to build breathtaking paths to my swimming hole on the creek. You get the idea.

Most importantly, don't let the tractors or anyone damage the features or materials that you can use for your macroscaping projects. Sometimes it's about getting the tractor in there and changing things and sometimes it's about keeping them away so they don't ruin something. I use the term "macroscaping" because it is the big picture that you are dealing with. Later, when you put in the lawn, shrubbery, the sidewalks and such, that is plain old landscaping, which can never enhance the beauty of what you can do to your country property by macroscaping!

One other aspect to macroscaping is that you are dealing with a huge piece of property and you need to capitalize on any free way to enhance the property that you can. I found that I could find free daffodil bulbs, iris bulbs, and native trees that I could transplant that would grow in the area without irrigation, which would make the property even more inviting and beautiful. Someone gave me an old manure spreader and some old gold mining junk one time, and I incorporated these into my property. This aspect of macroscaping should not be overlooked, as it presents an opportunity to give you a much nicer piece of property at no cost and truly raise its value for resale, if you ever decide to do so!

Grading the Home Site, Building the Road, and Installing Waterlines and Stuff

Now that you are prepared not to ruin a macroscaping opportunity, we can dig into actually tearing up the earth and getting your home site made, your barn pads in, your driveway built, and the waterlines and other underground stuff in. There is a process for this and some good things to keep in mind while you are doing this. You will want to check with your county departments to see if any permits will be needed. Some counties require permits for any underground electric and sewage lines, and almost all for septic systems, and most for wells. Our county even requires a permit for moving earth with a tractor if you move over a certain amount and you live in certain areas of the county! Just check with them; you should probably take your site plan in when you go to talk to them. If you have found an old grave, a caveman drawing, or some other such thing that might cause a problem with the bureaucrats, you might want to keep that between you and the proverbial fencepost so some genius who could throw a wrench into your plans doesn't get too carried away. They may require that you report such things in your area, but I am just saying!

Locating a good cat driver and tractor driver is the most important part of this phase. I already told you about my nightmare with the one cat driver and the boulders, so you know what we need at this point. We need someone who understands what we are after and has experience at developing country properties. There are always folks that specialize in this type of tractor work. You might ask your country property Realtor for some names, and he or she will most certainly be able to help you out. You can also ask some of the neighbors, and you might see some recent work that was done in the area that you liked and check into who did it. Usually, these country property tractor folks run their own equipment and have small businesses. I like to find someone that has newer equipment that is well taken care of, so they aren't broke down half the time, and someone who has a truck and trailer to haul their own equipment in and out if I can get it. If I am in rugged terrain or am going to move a lot of dirt and do a lot of work, I like to find someone with a large dozer, which usually must be hauled in by an equipment-moving company. You typically pay for the moving costs, so if it is a small job, it is better if the tractor operator can bring it in on his trailer, as this is usually free. No matter whom you use, and how good they claim to be, it is best to be there when they are working, if you can, and you should certainly explain how you want all boulders and other features to be preserved as much as possible, as well as point out specific features that are important to you.

Your cat driver should know it, but make sure your road is graded so the water runs from its center to the sides, and that it is built higher in the center ("crowned") so the road doesn't end up with water running down it when the road is going down a hill or it will need scads more maintenance. I can't count the number of gravel roads I drive where the gravel has washed off into the side of the road and made a dam, forcing even more water on the road, all because it was built wrong in the first place! Gravel roads always take maintenance, but the ones that traverse hills need ten times as much. A good, well-built gravel road built across flat terrain may last for years with almost no maintenance, where I have seen poorly built gravel roads on hills develop holes in them that you could lose a car in after just one rainy season.

Building a good driveway at first might cost you a little more, but you will save many times that over the years that you own the property. Having a nice, smooth road is easier on your vehicle tires and shocks as well, let alone your teeth and rear end! Make sure you install culverts that are big enough to handle the water flow that you expect. Your cat driver can help you with that, and usually you can just kind of tell what you think will work from looking at the drainage area you are crossing. If it is a small creek, and the banks are scoured up three feet, you are going to need a huge culvert, but if it is a little drain near the top of a hill that carries no water and you can barely see where the water runs in the grass, you will use a small and cheap one. I have seen folks actually hire an engineer for such things, and every time I have seen a molehill turn into a very expensive mountain that could have been avoided with a two-sentence conversation with any decent country property cat driver.

Keep in mind that the steeper the road, the more annual money you are going to spend on it for maintenance. Steep roads have more rainfall runoff no matter how well the road is constructed, and inevitably you and your guests' tires will spin in the gravel from time to time, making holes and mounds that will gather water and require grading often, or they will lead to substantial damage over time. Sometimes this is unavoidable, but there are times when you can build your road where it follows the contour of the property better, and you can avoid such maintenance costs.

Lastly, many counties and jurisdictions require that, for emergency vehicle access, any road over a thirty percent grade must be paved for that portion that does exceed this grade. Paving is very expensive, and this is another good reason to take care in choosing your home site, locating your driveway, and perhaps even in choosing which property you should buy. As with most issues, your county or jurisdiction might have no such requirement, or they may have a more stringent one, and you should check for the rules in the area that your property is located. You may even want to run this issue by your homeowner's insurance agent, as they may adjust their rates or have policies on driveway access. If your private road or driveway has a bridge over a creek, railroad tracks, or anything else, your insurance company may require that it be certified by a licensed engineer to carry the load of the typical fully loaded fire truck (about 30,000 pounds) in order to obtain insurance. Your county may have similar requirements prior to issuing a building permit as well.

When you develop your building site, it needs to be sloped so that it drains. Usually it only takes from about an eighth to a quarter inch downhill slope to each foot to get decent drainage. You certainly don't want big swimming pool puddles out your front door in your parking area, which I see a lot in my travels! You also want to make your building pad big enough for your home, yard, parking, driveway, sheds, garage, RV parking, and anything else you might have. A huge percentage of people underestimate their building pad's size and forever live in a cramped setting, playing "musical cars" every time someone comes or goes. They back into other cars and the garbage cans, and have to back up and go forward ten times to turn around. For this reason, I am a huge fan of having a circular drive at my country properties. Why not? You usually have the room!

When you do develop your building site, remember to keep your septic area in mind. If you haven't put it in yet, it should be downhill from your site so the sewage runs freely to it, or you will end up putting in a couple-thousand-dollar pumping station. Also, your septic area was probably looked at and approved and the county inspectors will not approve it if you fill it with loose soil or disturb it in some way. You also do not want to re-route water drainages near your septic tank and leach field area, as they make you stay back from these to prevent polluting them if your septic system has a problem; and putting a drainage closer might ruin your approved septic area.

I doubt you will have natural gas on your country property, as is common in town, so you might be planning to use propane or heating oil for your home rather than making it all electric. These usually require that they be set a little away from the home; they need larger pipes as they get farther from it, so keep their location in mind and make sure that you put them in your site plan.

When you are developing your home site or site for your shop, barn, or other improvements, keep your fire-clearing rules, property line setbacks, creek setbacks, and other county rules in your mind. Nowadays, you can really get your you-know-what in a ringer if you disturb a natural creek bank or wetlands (like I did in the example of macroscaping above) or some other sensitive environmental feature that exists on your land. This is a good time for you and the tractor driver to go over your site plan to determine such issues and refresh them in your mind.

Also, if you have big old trees around your site that are not healthy, now is the time to take them out, as having huge trees removed over your home can run thousands each, and your insurance agent might require this so they don't get stuck paying for your house repairs from a tree falling through it! Some trees are dangerous and messy and you want them out ASAP, anyway. Out here in our foothills, we have a big tree called a digger pine. They don't supply shade and they are huge, with ten-pound sappy pinecones in them that fall at random—they can kill you or ruin your house or car at any time—and the wood is too sappy to burn. Everyone removes these for sure, and you usually pull them up as seedlings so you don't have to deal with them later, as they grow like lightning! You will also want to remove any trees that have aggressive roots that are near your septic system at this point, as the roots can ruin them in a fraction of the time that they are expected to last.

Remember that when you move dirt around, and push it out over lower ground, you are "filling" that area. These areas where you fill will settle several inches and are unsuitable to be built upon unless they are properly compacted. Putting a foundation to a home or any building on this non-compacted fill is a huge mistake. This includes where you have dug out tree roots and boulders when you prepared your site. In many states, the building department will not allow you to build on fill unless it was compacted in about six-inch layers ("lifts") and tested by a soils engineer at each lift to assure that it was compacted to a point where no significant settling of the structure's foundation would occur, which is usually about ninety percent compaction or more. In areas that you aren't going to build on and there is fill, such as where you put your leach field lines in for your septic system, or places where you aren't too worried about a little settling, such as for a barn or shed, the tractor driver can compact these areas by rolling over them with his tractor or by you driving over them with your pickup tires over and over as you add just enough water to moisten the soil. You never want to add too much water so you get mud and the soil just squishes around, as this is anything but compaction!

Remember that when you are choosing your areas for your garden and livestock areas, they need to be close enough so that you can practically use them. You don't want to end up walking a hundred yards from the house twice a day to feed the livestock or grab a tomato. You don't want to put your livestock right on top of you where you are living, along with the smell, flies, and noises that come with them. You usually don't want your livestock area uphill from your home, either, as when the air cools it flows downhill and will carry all those organic aromas right to your dinner table! Critters like to eat your livestock, too, and the coons will be checking to see if you shut your chicken coop door every night and the occasional mountain lion or bobcat will want to make themselves at home, so being close enough to address these issues is important, too. Equally important is the fact all these areas will need water, power, or both, and the further they are from where these are, the more money it is going to cost you to supply them. This is a weigh-off that will be subject to the "lay of your land" to some extent, as on hilly ground, you might have room for your house on your hill and have to move to the next flat on the next knoll for the livestock, whether you like it or not.

Once you get all the flat spots ("pads") made for your house, barns, or other purposes, and your ground is right where you need it to be and is all compacted, now you tear it up again with trenches to put your underground water, electric, phone, and sewer lines in! You couldn't do this before because you didn't know how it was all going to turn out, and wouldn't have known how deep they needed to be. You don't want them ten feet deep, and some of them need to be a certain depth for building codes. You also want them protected from when you drive over them and work around them planting trees and such.

Next, you will head down to the electrical place and the water pipe sales place with good, accurate measurements that you stepped off with your very own two feet on how far you are going with each waterline and electrical line. These should be laid out in a map of your planned systems on a copy of your site plan. This is important because both electricity and water have something in common—the longer the run, the less water or electricity comes out the other end of the wire or pipe. With water, it is less water at less pressure; with electricity, you lose "voltage." Low voltage is hard on motors and electrical equipment, and the farther you go, the bigger the wire you need to prevent this loss to where it does damage. The electrical places have a book with a chart that shows you this, and I suggest that every one of you buy a book that I own and have used for many years called *Wiring Simplified*. I can't tell you how much I have learned and how much I use that book for reference when I do electrical work, and I do a lot of it. I have a huge house, and I wired it all myself to code, wired my well system, and put in my own meter, and this book was invaluable.

After you get your wire, buy any "subpanels" for the electrical that you need, as you should have a shut-off switch at each location, and you also should drive a copper grounding rod at each as well. Some folks say you don't need these grounds, but their job is to grab electricity that isn't where it should be, and if you are in a position where you are a better "ground" because the first ground rod in the system is way off back at the house, you will be wishing you had put one in! The building department might require this as well. Make sure you have planned both of these systems out thoroughly, as you don't want to be digging up your roads, pavement, and landscaping to add on later. If you plan to develop something later but don't want to spend the money on it now, just get the pipe, electrical conduit, and/or wire to it and set a temporary box in an area close by that area, called "stubbing out," for your future use.

Once all your trenches have the waterlines, electrical lines, gas lines, and whatever you needed in them, and you have had an inspection, if needed, you will "backfill" the trenches and compact them thoroughly with your pickup tire where any settling would be a problem. If you want, and it is in a key location, you can rent compactors that are the size of a big self-propelled lawn mower. These vibrate and beat the soil to compaction. Here again, a little bit of moisture and not too much is key. Often it is best to bring in sand to protect your water and electric lines if the ground is rocky.

Now, everything is leveled, graded properly for drainage, underground utilities are installed, everything is compacted, and you are ready to bring in some gravel and clean up the mess you made! You will have the tractor clean up the area best you can and remove any rocks that they can. You will pick some of them up by hand and dig some of the ones that are sticking up too far out so they don't stick up through the gravel. You will have the trucks come in and spread the gravel, and your tractor driver will spread and grade the gravel with the slope you need for drainage, much the same as you did when you prepped the ground earlier. Your place is starting to look like it is tame and the neighbors are impressed, while they put their two cents in on how they would have done it differently!

Can You Tell Me a Little About Septic Tanks So I Know What to Watch Out For?

Of course I can, and I will here in this section! We are going to make a country bumpkin out of your city slicker self yet!

Septic tanks are a low-maintenance device. You can go years with a properly installed septic system without even knowing it is any different from the city sewer in the town you came from. However, following a few simple rules can make them last a lot longer and with trouble-free operation.

A septic tank is a big, hollow box—usually plastic or concrete—that has two connected chambers. The raw sewage dumps into the first chamber at one end, and there are things floating on the top or sinking to the bottom, depending on what you had for dinner last night! The septic tank is a bacterial wonderland with little microorganisms running rampant throughout it, eating and composting all of the solids. As they are composted, they turn to liquid, and this liquid then flows through holes in the wall to the second chamber, which is located about halfway down towards the bottom where nothing is floating and nothing has sunk to.

On the other side, the composting continues, but the solids are long gone, for the most part. Each time someone runs water in the sink, the washer, or flushes the toilet, that water runs in side one and an equal amount leaves the tank on side two and goes to the leach lines. The leach lines are underground pipes that have holes in them that allow the water to leak into the soil over a large area. Ideally, much of this wastewater evaporates or is further dissolved and used by the surrounding plants for food. As I said, side one is alive with microorganisms, and you always want to avoid putting anything down the pipes and into the tank that is poison to these organisms, such as strong bleaches, lye, or cleaning products, as you will kill your little zoo. There are products that you can flush down your toilet that are little injections of these biological creatures to enhance your system, but if you are good to it, these are not necessary. Putting hard-to-dissolve things into your septic tank, such as meat, grease, and other solids, should be minimized. You usually don't put these things down the garbage disposal, anyway. A few egg shells, a little chicken skin, and the normal garbage disposal debris is fine.

Remember, your leach lines are pipes with little holes to let the water out. If your tank gets too full of solids, they can clog, and you would have to replace them. This is expensive, so it is not a bad idea to have you septic tank pumped by a septic company every five years or so, and make sure you keep trees with aggressive roots away from the leach lines. Tree roots are perhaps the number-one cause for leach line replacement, which costs about two grand! Pumping a septic tank is usually about a two- to four-hundred-dollar job, depending on the landfill fees and the size of your tank. The larger your home, usually by the bedroom count, the larger the septic tank that is required. They are usually between around 800 and 1500 gallons. If you ever think of adding a bedroom, make sure you size the tank accordingly when you put it in because there is not a huge difference in price for the larger tank, and the installation costs are about identical!

If your toilets don't flush and your sinks don't drain, or you see or smell sewage in the septic tank area, you may have a problem with your system. Sometimes the lines going in to the tank or coming out get crushed by tractors or vehicles during construction or later, and this is usually not too expensive to fix. One good way to check if your leach lines are failing is by removing the top to side two of the tank and looking at the pipe where the water exits to the leach lines. This pipe slopes downward and the water level should be at its very bottom. If it is "backed up" to where that pipe has water built up in it, there is an obvious obstruction. This can be a collapsed line from damage from vehicle traffic (you hope!), or it may indicate the water cannot leave the holes in the leach line and that they need to be replaced. Sometimes, your line is clogged where it leaves the house or under the house, and all you need is a plumber to "snake" the lines. If it is just one sink or toilet that is clogged, blame Uncle Fester's bowel movement, or maybe it is your lost cell phone!

Okay, Mr. Country Property, Tell Me about the Well!

As I said at the beginning of this book, having an adequate water well on any piece of country property that has no other alternative water source is absolutely essential. What is adequate will depend on your intended use of the property, but at a minimum, any property without a well that yields about three gallons of water a minute should be avoided. I don't mean three gallons a minute on a wet rainfall year in the midst of winter; I mean three gallons during the driest season of the year on a low rainfall year! Living on a property where you and the family alternate bath days, do laundry in town in a laundromat, and have no garden or landscaping possibilities is not a life that I think you would find enjoyable. Hopefully, you purchased property with a productive well that produces water that is suitable for drinking, but if you did end up with a low-yielding well or a well that has some quality issues, I will also tell you a little about your alternatives in these cases a little later.

To begin with, a well is simply a hole in the ground. That hole can be anywhere from twenty feet to more than a thousand, and the twenty-foot well might produce a hundred times as much water as the one that is a thousand feet. Some older wells (and there are a lot of them in use) that are less than fifty feet were often hand dug and resemble the pictures in your old Hansel and Gretel storybook, with the rock stacked on the sides of it in a circle to the bottom. After all, many home sites were in place since shortly after Columbus stumbled upon our country in 1492, and modern well-drilling equipment didn't surface until the late 1800s and wasn't used popularly until the early 1900s. For the most part, I am going to talk about the typical machine-drilled wells, but as I talk about shallow wells and the typical way that water is pumped from them and the concerns that you should have about shallow or older wells, those principles will be applicable to these old hand-dug wells also. After all, they are all just simply holes in the ground, and the concerns and ways to get the water up and out are all the same!

You Mentioned Water Quality —
What Should I Be Concerned About?

Just because you have a lot of water doesn't mean that you are home free as far as water goes. The quantity is one part of the equation, and quality is the other key factor. Most of the time, well water is fairly good water for drinking and other purposes, but often it may have some discoloration or aroma that you may want to address. Many wells are coming from an area where the water interacts in some way with the minerals in the ground and takes on some of their characteristics. Usually these minerals will be harmless to your health and may even have some benefits. Many wells in the country will have the smell of sulfur, which smells of rotten eggs and takes some getting used to. After a while, when you turn the faucet on for your morning shower or coffee, you will become accustomed to the sensation that someone just passed gas in your face! Usually, this smell dissipates as more and more water is run through the system, and your local water filtration companies can help you filter or hide much of this smell. Another very common mineral in well water is iron. Iron usually doesn't have an odor, however, it is often found in wells that also have sulfur content. Iron's negative character is that it is basically a "rust" and has that rusty color in your water glass and in your washing machine. You may live with drinking a little rusty-looking water that may supply you with your daily iron needs, but your family might not like always wearing the same reddish, rust-colored, off-white clothes! You may also not like the look of that same color in your showers, toilets, and sinks. Also, where there are minerals, you usually have "hard" (mineralized) water that can cause a build-up in your showerheads and waterlines, as well as on your shower doors, shower floors, and toilets and sinks. A water "softener" might need to be installed, which isn't overly expensive, and it takes little maintenance to address this hard water. You may need to install other filtration equipment for the iron and other minerals. These are very common water issues, which are usually more of an inconvenience than a huge problem.

Probably the biggest concern with having a well is a common bacterium called coliform. This little microscopic beast is nothing overly dangerous and very easy to rid from your system. Many folks that live in the country have this bacteria present in their well and don't even know it. Their bodies are accustomed to it, and only Aunt Beatrice seems to spend an inordinate amount of time in the bathroom with a case of the "trots" when she visits from the city! If you set a glass of water on your windowsill for a period of time, it will probably develop a coliform population. Put a drop of bleach in the glass and they are gone! This is true with your water system as well—albeit a little more of a process, and more than a drop of bleach is needed. Any newly drilled well, a well that has been sitting without much use, and most wells over a period of time will more than likely develop a need to be decontaminated for coliform bacteria.

The typical process for doing this is to dump chlorine bleach or tablets down the well and run every faucet, flush every toilet, run the dishwasher, and use a hose to squirt down the little "inspection" hole on the top of the well itself so the bleach makes its way throughout your entire water system, and so the pipe in your well itself gets a thorough shower. You can tell when you have adequately run enough water through each faucet, as you should smell the chlorine at each. Once the whole system is full of the chlorine water, let it sit for 24 hours or so (at least overnight), and then run every faucet, shower, hose, etc. until you do not smell chlorine any longer. That should take care of the problem, but you can have it re-tested at a cost of usually under a hundred bucks to make sure. I usually treat any new system or one that I am new to right off the bat, and then test it after so I don't have to pay for two tests. Usually, in many areas, the county requires that you decontaminate new wells in this way and has instructions on how to do so on a handout in their office. How much chlorine to use depends on the depth of the well and the size of your entire system. However, I have done mine a hundred times, and I usually just dump a gallon or two down the well and just make sure I flush it out well. Make sure you put little notes at the shower and faucets so the family doesn't drink it and so that the wife doesn't show up at work the next day with white or red hair!

A more concerning problem is when you have the well tested and it has the presence of "fecal" coliform bacteria. This bacterium is not as common, but definitely is not uncommon. Of the wells that I have had tested in my real estate career on country properties that had existing homes on them, perhaps around two to five percent of them had a fecal coliform problem, where as nearly twenty-five percent of them had a regular coliform issue. Fecal coliform is much more dangerous to the health, as it originates from some contamination from the "poop" of people or farm animals. Many times this is just an abnormal event that might be cured with bleach, but oftentimes this is an indication of a problem that will be ongoing and must be addressed in some way, even if it involves drilling a new well! Typical sources of this type of contamination are runoff water from pastures, barns, kennels, or other animal enclosures or from a septic system that is either too close to the well or not functioning properly, with the sewage making its way to the surface — and that includes from some adjoining neighbor's property. Often, a main reason for this contamination is a combination of one of these factors, along with the fact that the well has no "surface seal," which would have prevented such a contamination even in the event of it being affected by one of these factors. Regardless, this issue needs to be investigated and remedied, and please take my advice here with a grain of salt, as I am not a contamination specialist or water expert!

Well seals are an important feature to prevent such contamination, as well as to prevent unfiltered rain and snow runoff from flowing down into your well. A well seal is simply when the top thirty to one hundred feet of the hole is sealed with concrete or an expanding clay (bentonite clay, usually) around the pipe that goes into the ground to keep the sides of the well from caving in (the "casing") so that it doesn't let water pass through it. The hole for the well is drilled and the pipe is put down the hole and then the hole is filled up with "pea gravel" to where the seal is to start, and then the concrete or clay is poured on top of this gravel to the surface. Some jurisdictions don't require well permits, and you aren't required to do this, but I think it is a huge and non-correctable mistake not to do this!

Some jurisdictions (counties, or whatever they call them in your state) require such a seal, and they MUST be present when you do it, and they have a certain depth that is required for a seal. They come out for the sealing process and stick a tape measure on the outside of the pipe until it hits that pea gravel. They make sure it is at least what they require in depth, and then watch you pour in the clay or concrete to the surface. DO NOT put too much gravel in the hole and make the seal area less than what is required, or you will be figuring out how to get down there to get some of that gravel out, and I doubt you have that long of an arm to hold the teaspoon scoop down there! If you live on a dairy farm or have other livestock in the area, or you have gravelly soil down to a certain level where it lets the surface water readily flow into the well, a deeper well seal is desirable. Sealing to the first impervious layer is a good idea in these cases. Talk this over with a well driller in your area and the county health department, as they are the experts that can help you. If your well is the old Hansel and Gretel type with the bucket hanging over it, you may not have many options, and, as with any shallow well, you will more than likely run into these problems much more often than with deeper wells.

I won't elaborate too much, but there are other contaminants that you should be aware of as well, and the county health department, well drillers, and pump installers will probably be aware of any concerns in your area. I sold one property that had an unusual amount of bicarbonate soda in the well, which had a high salt content and was neither good for drinking or watering plants. Some areas near landfills or in areas where there were old gold mines and other industrial activities might have their own set of problems, such as PCBs, mercury, or diesel fuel. There are water-testing laboratories that can test for anything you desire, but it is best to know what to be suspect, as having them test for every conceivable contaminant could run you tens of thousands of dollars. After all, why test for some chemical that is only found in the far reaches of Siberia?

What About the Well Pump and the Rest of the Water System?

I am going to start by telling you how the typical well water system works and what its components are and then move to a little explanation of how to set your system up if you don't have enough water, and then a few trouble-shooting hints that you should know before you call the pump guy out.

First, every system needs a pump to get the water out of the ground and to pressurize it so your showers and faucets work in the house. Most well pumps are down at the bottom of the pipe that is down in the well and are called "submersible" pumps. They have wire all the way down to them running alongside the pipe. They are not so deep in the well hole that they are right at or near the bottom, or you would be stirring up mud all the time, and if the well filled in with a little dirt or gravel, they would be ruined. The pump usually sits up at least twenty feet or more from the bottom of your well. The pipe down the hole is either plastic or metal, and if it is a deeper hole, the plastic is a thicker type that screws together rather than glues, so it can be pulled out in sections if you need to work on the hole. In some cases, to save money when the hole is shallow, the pump is clamped onto a thick rubber hose that is all one piece and can be pulled out as one piece and laid across the ground. Many times this is actually done by hand and by the homeowner to save money. Metal pipe and the heavy plastic pipe are pulled out in sections using a small truck with a hoist that is made for that purpose.

There is usually a "check valve" above every submersible pump down in the well that only lets the water go in one direction, and when the pump shuts off, the valve closes and doesn't allow the water in the pipe to drain back down into the well, as well as all the water in your entire system, including the house! The pipe itself is fitted with odd-looking rubber bumpers for the first fifty to hundred feet or so, and these bumpers are critical if you ever decide to install your own pump, like I do a lot. These bumpers are actually "shock absorbers" that inhibit the pipe from twisting and jerking in the hole when the pump kicks on. Your wire is taped to the pipe and is inside the slits in these bumpers. Without them, the pipe can wear out against the casing, the wires can get the insulation rubbed off and short out, or the pump can come loose off of the pipe altogether! This is why every submersible pump has a place for a nylon rope to be tied to it so the rope can run to the surface and the pump can be recovered if it were to come loose off the pipe or the pipe breaks in half. Never forget this rope, as pumps are expensive! Just so you know, the pump in the hole actually has two parts, and they can be replaced separately to save some money, but this is usually not the best idea, as if one part is worn out, the other is probably well on its way, and you may have just paid dearly to have a pump guy pull the pipe out when you might want to kill two birds with one stone. The actual pump is one of these parts and is on the top of the pump assembly, while the motor is the other and sits on the bottom of the assembly and powers the pump. I just didn't want your know-it-all friend to say I forgot something!

Once the water comes out of the ground, it goes into a "pressure tank," which is the big blue tank you see sitting on the property of everyone who hasn't got around to building their well house yet. The pressure tank is a holding tank whose job is to fill up with water when the pump turns on until it gets so full that the air in the tank gets compressed enough that it can supply water under pressure to your home while the pump is not running. The reason you don't want your pump to turn on every time you turn on a faucet is that the more times a pump turns on and off, the faster it wears out and needs to be replaced, and as I said, they are expensive. The average family of four uses about four hundred gallons of water a day for household purposes, so if you have an eighty-gallon pressure tank, your pump may kick on just five times a day for those purposes as opposed to every time a toilet flushes or somebody gets a drink of water or washes their hands.

If you irrigate your lawn or trees or what have you, try to use enough water where your pump runs as continually as possible to make it last longer. An abused pump might last ten percent of the time that you would expect. It is not uncommon for a pump to last well over ten years. The larger your pump, the larger the tank (or number of tanks) you should have. Your pump guy can help you with this, as there is an actual chart for such a decision. Your pump should be sized for your planned use and for the amount of water that your well produces, and the pump company will help you with this, too.

Your water system includes a "pressure switch" that tells the pump in the tank when to turn on and pump more water into the pressure tank. A typical house needs to operate with water pressure between thirty pounds minimum and sixty pounds maximum, and your tank should be filled until the air in it is compressed to sixty pounds, where your pump is set to turn off. Your pump should kick back on when that pressure falls to about thirty pounds. The pressure switches are set at the factory for this range and only rarely need adjustment. Most pressure tanks these days are of the "bladder bag" type that actually have a rubber bag in them to keep the water separate from the air in the tank so the tank doesn't lose air and become full of water where no pressure can build up, which causes the pump to kick on every time you turn on a faucet just as if the pressure tank didn't exist!

If you have a regular galvanized tank that has no air in it, or you have a faulty or broken bladder in your tank and it is full of water, you will notice that instead of the well kicking on once every hour or two, it turns on and off every five minutes, or whenever you turn on a faucet. This is called being "waterlogged" and it needs to be addressed right away to save the massive wear and tear on your pump. With a non-bladder bag type galvanized tank, you simply shut the power to the well off and drain your entire water tank, opening the air valve somewhere on the tank to let the entire tank refill with air. Then close the air valve and turn the power on, and you will be good until the next time—and there will be a next time, as this is normal maintenance that should be religiously done on such non-bladder systems.

If your bladder bag system is broken and waterlogged, you can replace it or you could just use it like the one I described above and maintain it regularly as such. It is very important for you to know that all bladder bag tanks have an air fill on them that is identical to the one on your bicycle or car tire. They need to have a very specific amount of air in them to operate properly and optimally, and are supposedly set at the factory, which is rarely true! You should always consult your paperwork or give the pump folks a call and find out what they are to be set at when empty and check this with a standard air gauge that you would use on your car tire. You can then either add air or remove air to set them at their proper level. If there is too much air, they hold almost no water; too little air causes them to hold too much, which can cause your rubber bladder to pop like a balloon! In either case, your pump will be working overtime and wearing out until you fix this. Make sure you check this even if the pump guys installed it, as they seem to have a tendency to overlook this part of their job most of the time.

There are other electrical items, such as the "control box," which is that one other box at the well that has capacitors in it that can shock you even when the electricity is off, but all you really need to know is that it is easy to put in yourself with the directions and, most importantly, that it has hidden, usually on its bottom, a "reset" button that oftentimes will be all you need to do when your well stops functioning and you are in a panic. Most folks don't even know it's there and spend money on a well pump company to rush out on a service call and push it for you (and not tell you what the problem was). There, I just saved you ten times more than you paid for this book, so you owe me!

Speaking of problems, another problem that often occurs that the homeowner can check is insects in the pressure switch. Insects seem to enjoy crawling into the "points" (little electrical contacts) in the pressure switch. Often cleaning these with a fingernail emery board will fix your problem, but BE CAREFUL! These points carry 220 volts of electricity! Turn off the juice and consult your manual or an electrician!

For shallower wells, those less than forty or fifty feet, it is very common to use an above-ground "jet" pump. These are usually about the size of a lawnmower engine and sit on the ground at the well. These are very affordable, easy to change if they go bad, and are fine where the water isn't too deep, as they can only "lift" it so high efficiently. They pressurize the pressure tank the same way, and everything else works the same as well.

Other than having a main water valve to shut off all the water to your property if needed, as well as a switch at the well to shut off all the power to the well, and then some valves to each system, such as the house, the garden, the barn, etc., you are pretty much done. However, I will point out one thing that I see over and over that bugs the living you-know-what out of me. When you drill a well, the county usually requires that you pour some concrete around the pipe in about a six-foot-square slab as part of the well seal and to stabilize the pipe. The new gentleman farmer who forgot to read this book will inevitably use that concrete slab to build his needed well house upon. Then when the well has a problem and the pipe has to come out, there is a frickin' building in the way! Build your well house out of the way and always leave an access road area for the pump truck, which is big, to get to your well. I partially blame the pump companies for this issue, as ninety-nine point nine times out of a hundred they will put all the electronics right on that slab, and protecting them with a building seems like the thing to do. Prepare for your well, and pour a second slab for your well house, and make it big enough for other purposes while you are at it!

What If My Well Produces Very Little Water—
Can You Help Me?

You are in luck, but plan on spending some money to make your water system adequate for some degree of living, but perhaps not for all of your intended uses. If your well's water yield is extremely low, you may have to forgo or curtail some of the activities and uses that you had planned so you have enough for the house and living purposes. Trust me, having water for your morning coffee is much more important than for watering a weeping willow tree that drinks a hundred gallons a day! If your water yield is too low, there is very little you can do short of crossing your fingers and drilling another well or cutting some deal with your neighbor who has a good well. Be aware, too, that in many jurisdictions, the building department may not allow the issuance of a building permit if the well does not produce a certain minimum amount of water. In our area, that amount is three gallons per minute, which is a huge reason to be suspect of well reports that are near this amount of yield. I say this because many well drillers will "fudge" their test results a little to help a landowner with this issue when asked or begged to do so by a landowner.

As I mentioned earlier, the average family uses an estimated hundred gallons of water per day, per person. My teenage daughter uses all four of our shares in one shower! If your well is a low-yielding well, let's say a gallon per minute, that adds up to sixty gallons per hour, and therefore almost fifteen hundred gallons a day. This is about the minimum that is acceptable under any circumstance, and that is only if your water system has a big storage tank (or tanks) to store it as you extract it out of the well, which we are going to discuss momentarily.

This is a livable amount, but if your toilet runs unless you jiggle the handle, you have a leaky faucet, or somebody leaves the hose running outside for any period of time, any of these can be wasting two or three gallons a minute from your storage tank, and in a matter of a half of a day or so, you are out of water and you have to shut everything off, let the water have time to "build" back up, and then "re-prime" your water pump and system. I am not going to discuss re-priming here in this book, but just let me say that it is not necessarily difficult, but it does take five or ten minutes and is a pain in the butt! This is especially true if some member of the family or a guest is the only one home, and that person is unfamiliar with the process, which varies from system to system. Trust me, the significant other will not like the pump-priming process or going without the water! For any low-water system, I recommend having at least a fifteen-hundred-gallon storage tank. Be advised right now that the more storage you have, the more pleasant and hassle-free your life will be. Right now, you can plan on paying about fifty cents per gallon of storage for large plastic tanks.

I want you to follow me on this, as this is a simple concept that is important to understand if you have a low-yielding well. Your water pump and system will be the same as a regular one, as I described above, except in the well you will have a switching device to tell your pump when to turn on because there is enough water that has built up in the well hole to make it worth starting the pump for a while. When the water in the well then pumps out to where it is low in the well, this switch tells it to turn off. Water pumps are cooled by the well water, and if they sit and run without water in them, they will quickly burn up and be ruined! This is true for both submersible and aboveground pumps.

As this water is pumped up, it needs to go into your big storage tank for use when you need it. This big tank has a switch that sends a message down to the pump that says, "Hey, I am getting low, keep sending me water when you can until I get full." So, as water leaks into the well from the ground to a desired point, the pump turns on and off, over and over when it can, until the tank up top lets it know that it is full and there is no need to send any more.

Now, your big tank in such a system "becomes the well" for purposes of the second half of this low-water system that I will describe now! You have an aboveground "jet" pump that is connected to the big tank in addition to the one in the well. Now you have a pressure tank and a pressure switch and everything identical to a normal well, except that the water is coming from your big tank instead of the well! Again, take care not to use all the water in this big tank or you will be in the "priming" situation we just talked about. This system is pretty simple, really, and any good pump company that is used to helping folks with low-water situations will be able to set this up for you—albeit at a cost of a few thousand over that of a normal well system. But, at least you have water, to some degree.

Section III

How to Be a Good Country Neighbor and Some Country Living Hints

Section III — How to Be a Good Country Neighbor and Some Country Living Hints

Great, You Got Me Here! Any Hints for Being a Good Country Neighbor?

I'm so glad you asked that question. Now I won't have to go postal on you if you are my neighbor!

When you move to the country, it is important to be a good neighbor in many respects that would not apply in an in-town setting. Certainly many, if not all, of the same neighborly practices that you employ in neighborhoods in the cities apply in rural settings, but some become even more important, while others will be new types of kindnesses that you should embrace. Of course the "golden rule" of treating others how you would want to be treated is still the most important guiding principle, but you may not realize just exactly what this entails in a country setting. I have lived in the country for most of my sixty-year life, and I have come to learn a lot about country etiquette. I will share my two-cents on some of the most important aspects of it below.

Dog Etiquette!

My Uncle Malcolm Benjamin lived in the country his whole life and was a good, honest man that truly cared about how he treated his neighbors. As a matter of fact, he once told me right before he died, "You know, Coop, when you die, the only thing that ever really mattered was good food, your family, and your friends." He lived in the country in a somewhat isolated area, and his friends were primarily his neighbors, and they respected him. I tell you this because he shared something else with me that, while it seemed odd when I was young, came to be the truest thing I ever learned about being a good neighbor in the country, and that was that "good fences make good neighbors."

In the country, probably the most problematic issue between neighbors is dogs. Some folks love their dogs like their children, while others simply don't care for them at all. When you move to the country, you don't see many solid wooden fences like you do in town, and nearly everyone has dogs for security and friendship. Many folks that are new to the country lifestyle rush out and get dogs as one of their first acts to begin their country dream, and they may not have a clue to what owning dogs is all about. What you do see is folks that have no fencing or wire livestock fencing that is made to hold cows and horses in, and the person's dogs stay at home out of their own loyalty and training. However, when the neighbor's dog down the street is in heat or just wanders by to socialize and explore, or a landowner is off at work all day or leaves town for a couple of days and his dogs get bored and wander, some huge neighbor issues often arise.

Many folks in the country have chickens, cats, cows, sheep, and other livestock that they cherish or make their living from. When your dogs wander into their yards, they all have varying degrees of tolerance and might take any number of actions, from throwing rocks at them to shooting them on the spot, even though they may have done no harm. If your dogs chase their livestock or kill their chickens, which happen a lot, they may scare them off and come talk to you or just shoot them and hang them on their fence out where you will be driving by when you are coming home or are out looking for them. In most states and counties, this is completely legal, and in many areas the courts will make you pay for any damages caused by your dogs, as well as a sizeable fine! If someone does shoot your dogs on their property, my advice is to "suck it up" and realize that you should have controlled your dogs and built better fences for their protection and control.

If your neighbor doesn't shoot your dogs and comes to talk to you about them, be respectful and take immediate action, as when they "invade" his property they disrupt his lifestyle on his own "Garden of Eden." Not doing so makes you officially a nightmare neighbor! Even if a neighbor says in a kind and casual way that "your dogs came by for a visit today," you should immediately apologize and take action, as even if they don't truly mind, the next neighbor will, and your dogs are in great peril!

If any of your neighbors truly like your dogs and they or their children feed them, let them in their house, play with them, or anything besides scold them and send them home, they are "training" your dogs to run away, and you need to have a talk with them for the sake of your dogs. Invite them up to visit your dogs or offer to walk them by occasionally, but stress to them how they can help you keep them safe by telling them to "GO HOME" and by throwing rocks at them instead. Throwing rocks at your dogs in the country is an act of kindness, as far as I am concerned. You don't throw them to hit them, necessarily, but at least so they know that they could have been hit. Handfuls of gravel are great for this, as you can hit them enough to get the point across but not harm them. Also, you should always stop and throw rocks and scold if at any time your dogs begin to follow your car out of the driveway. They need to know where home is and to stay at it!

One of the best and most effective tools for containing your dogs is the electronic collars they sell with the "invisible fence." With these, you simply run an inexpensive single wire around where you want the dog to stay (which can be buried), put the collar on the dog, plug the fence in, and if the dog gets near the wire, they get a shock. These collars vibrate prior to shocking the dog so they learn to stop very soon when they feel this. You might run a temporary visible marker around the area so they can see this imaginary line as well so they relate to the boundary in a physical way. This is an acceptably humane way to safeguard your dogs at a reasonable cost.

Also, you will sooner or later have some interaction on your property with the neighbor's dogs, and you should throw rocks and scare them off. Do them a favor and share your invisible fence idea with your neighbor, and let them know that they were at your place at least. If you do shoot some irresponsible neighbor's dog, my advice is to keep that between you and the fencepost and just tell the little white lie that you haven't seen it unless you're found out. At least make an effort for the dog's sake to correct the situation as much as you can, though, because it is not the dog's fault. You may even consider taking the dog to a new owner out of the area or to the humane society so they have to pay to get it out and start controlling it for that reason alone. For cats, suck it up and live with it—they're cats!

Other Livestock Considerations to Think About...

When you move to the country, you are usually ready to become that gentleman farmer you always wanted to be and start your herd of horses, cattle, sheep, chickens, turkeys, llamas, goats, and other critters that tickle your fancy. There is certainly nothing wrong with that, but use your head for something other than a hat rack for that new cowboy hat you're sporting! Get your fences in place permanently so they are built specifically for the type of livestock that you plan to get before you get them. Horses in a small area do best with a wooden or metal pole-type fence, and in pastures and larger areas, the "field" type fencing is typical for both horses and cows. To contain either in any type of enclosure, use an electric wire on it for best results. If your neighbor's fence is already in place, treat it with great respect by using an electric wire on it or putting your own fence in front of it. Remember, too, their fence is probably a few inches inside their property and it was bought and paid for by them. If you would like to use it because it is there and practical and obviously being used by that neighbor for the same purpose, talk to them about it and offer to "electrify" your side for your animals and make any repairs to damages caused by your animals. If no fence exists, you might offer to build it and split the cost and discuss what you both should do to protect it from damage. If your neighbor's house is close to your property line, show respect by not placing your pigsty, barn, or chicken coop right at his or her bedroom window. If your neighbor has a garden and landscaping, you want to try and keep your chickens in your fenced barnyard so they don't wipe their new vegetables out before they even get started.

Your pigpen should be solid as a rock and be able to hold a large pig in. Their necks are strong, and when they are full-grown they can pull a fencepost up, concrete and all, if they get a hankering to do so, and they can wipe out a garden in minutes. Animals are also loud, so keep this factor in mind when locating your pens.

Notice, too, that every one of these considerations applies to your own property. You might find that your wife's ire far outpaces your neighbor's when her garden is eaten by your hogs! These fences will also keep the neighbor's dogs from killing your chickens and other critters, which is a huge benefit. Once again, "good fences make for good neighbors."

Make Sure You Drive Slowly and Courteously (And That Goes for Your Guests, Too!)

Another one of the major country neighborhood conflicts arises due to you or your guests speeding up and down the roads. Gravel roads are dusty, they require maintenance, and they are not as safe as paved roads. The drive to your house might be quite a long drive, but your hurry should never trump your neighbors' rights to enjoy their neighborhood, cost them money, or endanger them or their pets. Dust in the country is always an issue, but some neighbor speeding up and down your gravel road is an uncalled for assault on your enjoyment. Have some respect and make sure your guests do as well, as many city folks tend to speed, and in their minds they are crawling at a snail's pace. Putting up some "SLOW – DUST" signs for your neighbors and you is always courteous and helpful. Slower traffic causes less damage to the roads. Braking and steering on gravel roads can also be tricky, and your neighbor or his children might be in the roadway, and speeding really raises the risk that someone could get hurt or worse.

One of the worst abuses of your neighbor, as far as the road is concerned, is when you move to the country and you or your kids think that your shared road is a race track or practice area for their motorcycles, cars, or go carts. I have seen this cause major neighbor issues, and rightfully so. You are in the country, so there is probably some riding area to be enjoyed close by. Here again, a little respect is in order. Also, avoid parking vehicles in the roadway, drive courteously if you meet someone on the road, especially if it is a one-lane road. Repair any damage your family or guests do immediately and let it be known that you are a willing participant in maintaining the road.

Enjoy the Peace and Quiet of the Country — And Let Your Neighbors Do the Same

When most folks move to the country, they are looking forward to getting out of the hustle-bustle of the city, and that includes getting away from the noise. If you come in and set your shop up and start working on your race car and revving its engine late at night regularly, run a generator at all hours, let your dog bark all night, or make a habit of screaming at your spouse or kids all day long within earshot of your neighbors, you are not going to be very welcome in the neighborhood. If you live in an area of midsized parcels (smaller than forty acres), I can promise that shooting guns regularly will make your neighbors unhappy and uncomfortable. Besides the noisy disruption to the area, there is no telling what kind of gun you are shooting or which direction it is pointed. You may teach hunters' safety courses at the school, but when you start shooting in a country neighborhood, the tacit assumption of all the neighbors is that the gun is either pointed in their direction or in such a way that the ricochet will come that way. Also, on smaller parcels, there is no way to tell who is where at any one time, especially in woodsy or hilly areas. Shooting some critter from time to time or even killing a deer might be acceptable in season, but continual shooting will be frowned upon. People often get touchy about the critters in the neighborhood, and it is courteous to let them be. Many times folks feed the local deer, quail, and other critters, and it isn't going to kill you to take a drive and hunt elsewhere. I know this, as I hunt a lot and I have suffered through letting some trophy bucks meander through my yard to the neighbors! Actually, I even enjoy their visits in my old age!

Enjoy Your Privacy in the Country, and Let the Neighbors Bask in Theirs, Too!

Perhaps one of the biggest reasons that folks move to the country is to enjoy their privacy. It is a good idea to not make a habit of just dropping in on the neighbors, even if they invite you to do so. Doing this might imply an open invitation to do the same to you, and sometimes folks become a tad too friendly to downright being pests. It is good to get your neighbor's phone number, anyway, for a number of reasons, and to make a habit of calling them when you plan to drop by. They will then usually afford you the same courtesy. When you are wandering around the neighborhood or hiking, stay off other folks' land unless you have permission to traverse it, and make this practice clear with your children. When you develop your property, and your neighbor's home and property is private due to trees and brush, there is an almost certain probability that they will deeply appreciate you leaving that visual barrier if there is any way possible; and when you choose your home site, try to keep your distance. Keeping this separation will be important when you go to sell your property; even though it may not be important to you, the average country property buyer will reject property that is not private.

Another big aspect of respecting privacy of the neighbors is to not get involved in neighborhood disputes and gossip. At some time, one of your neighbors is going to share some juicy details with you about the other neighbors, which is true of about any neighborhood, including in town. It is best to be polite and respond as though this is not of any interest to you whatsoever—no matter how juicy the detail is and how bad you yearn to hear the whole story—and change the subject. If the neighbors are having a dispute, they will often want you to mediate or take sides, and I can promise you that no matter which side you choose, it is the losing one! Don't be afraid to smile and politely make it clear that, out of respect for both that neighbor in front of you and the one that is not, that you don't want to be involved. If the neighbor shares some fact with you that could cause a "blow up" in the neighborhood, such as that he shot the other neighbor's dog, I suggest you keep it to yourself unless it is something certain and proven that everyone should know, such as that they stole something from the other person, and then everyone should know. Just go out of your way to be independent and mind your own business when possible.

Any Other Helpful Hints on Being a Good Country Neighbor?

Yep, a couple more quick ones do come to mind.

One is to take care borrowing tools and equipment from the neighbor. If you do, return it immediately, clean, full of fuel if applicable, and in the same condition as you got it. When you borrow something, agree with yourself right on the spot that if it breaks, you will pay to have it repaired or replaced no matter the cost. Many a good relationship between neighbors has been ruined by not following these simple rules. If you are one of those folks that never gets around to returning tools in a timely manner, do not borrow them!

Another touchy subject that arises quite often when you buy country property that can cause problems is opting to use, or not use, your neighbor for tractor work, construction, or some other service that you need. This is one of those "damned if you do, damned if you don't" situations. Often one of your neighbors has a backhoe, tractor, or some expertise in some service that you obviously need. They may be in the business of that particular trade, have a stellar reputation, be properly insured, and offer you a fair price for their services. In this case, you may choose to have them help you out with some degree of comfort. However, more often than not, some neighbor will own some junk piece of semi-antique equipment that leaks hydraulic oil at a pace that no one can afford to support, and they have an amount of experience running it that they believe has made them an expert, when in reality their lack of expertise is going to cost you a fortune in extra time for any job. This fine specimen of equipment will be broke down and waiting on parts much of the time that you are trying to accomplish something, and your neighbor will be looking for a little "advance" so as to buy the new part or his whisky! Trust me, this is a totally common scenario and a sticky one. Saying no can leave him at the least a little butt hurt. Saying yes will cost you money, delay your job, leave you frustrated, and you will be the butt-hurt individual. Here, I am going to strongly recommend that you leave him butt hurt! You can be tactful and let him know you already promised some work to a friend of a friend that can use the money, and then get on the horn right away to your tractor driver that you have never met and explain the situation so he can "play along"!

Also, when someone works on your property, there is a chance that they will get hurt. If you have a licensed contractor on the job, you will have protection in this case, and if he has employees, you want to have him verify that he has workman's compensation insurance or some type of similar insurance in case the employee gets hurt. You should also check with your insurance agent and see how best to cover yourself for these contractors, or any of your helpers.

One other neighborly thing that you can do for all your neighbors is keep your place neat and free of junk, debris, old cars, and keep it in a generally attractive condition. One pack rat with every junk boat, car, or motor home that was offered to him, or a bunch of pens and cages made from junk wire and pallets, will subtract many thousands in property value from every neighbor in the area. Even though you have the room for all your friends to store their restoration projects, avoid doing so and make your best effort to keep a clean appearance from the neighbors' houses and the road where their guests drive.

Any Other Good Ideas to Make My Country Living Smoother and Safer?

Did you have to ask? I do have some other helpful hints and thoughts for you.

At the top of the list is having some emergency supplies on hand. When you live in the country and it is quite a jaunt to town, you need to be prepared for a number of things. You should have a complete first-aid kit for sure, and this should always include antihistamines, which are often overlooked and thought of as medicine for a stuffy nose. Antihistamines are a critical first-aid medicine for wasp stings, bee stings, snakebites, and allergic reactions to foods and other things you or your guests might come into contact with. When away from medical help, if someone has an allergic reaction to anything, whether or not you have antihistamines on hand could mean saving their lives or losing them. You should also be prepared to give your dogs antihistamines as well for snakebites. My friend lives in a rattlesnake-infested area in the hills, and their vet just has them give their dogs antihistamines as their complete treatment for snakebites, and their dogs have survived every time. Another friend of mine took their dog in to the vet, and their cost was just under two thousand dollars. My dog better have good luck with antihistamines or it is screwed!

You also need to "be prepared" for beyond just medical emergencies. In the country, oftentimes a tree branch will fall somewhere in the miles of electrical lines that run out to your property, a car will hit a pole, or some other factor will cause your power to go out—often for an extended period of time. Most country property folks own a generator for these times. Just be careful when you hook it up to your house, though, because if you don't turn off the breaker so your house is still hooked into the electrical lines, your electricity will be feeding back into the lines and could shock your neighbors or the workers who are working to repair the electrical lines. They do make a special panel to safely use a generator in your home, so you don't have to know much about electricity to connect a generator safely.

If a huge storm is rolling in, you might consider filling your bathtubs up with water and maybe putting some buckets under the rain gutters. This water comes in handy if you need to flush your toilets and the electricity to your well is out.

It's always good to have some food and drinking water in the pantry. If the road to town or some bridge gets washed out, you will be glad you had the foresight to do so—not to mention if there is an earthquake, flood, terrorist attack, or some other disaster. You should be able to survive at least a month or so on your emergency supplies, and don't forget to stock up for the dogs, cats, and the other critters, too. It also never hurts to have extra gasoline stocked away, as I guarantee that you will forget to fill up your car sooner or later and wake up to go to work on empty! So will your neighbor, and they will be there to borrow it from you. Same with propane gas—have a little extra around for when you unexpectedly run out or if there is some catastrophic event that occurs. Also, always have fire extinguishers handy in your home, in your shop, and in any outbuildings you might have. Unlike in town, you may be some distance from the firehouse, and a fire extinguisher could save your place from burning down.

Okay, "Mr. Country Property," Got Any Helpful Hints for Maintaining Such a Big Property?

Now this I can help you with. I have been doing this my whole life, and I have done it all the hard way because my book wasn't out yet for me to read! Over time, I have learned the key tools and tricks for keeping country property neat and "groomed" without spending too much money on hiring help or working myself to death. The tools that I have found essential are:

- A riding lawn tractor (18 horsepower or more)

- A good gas-powered weed eater, and not some cheap brand (I like Stihl and Husqvarna,)
- A three-gallon backpack weed sprayer
- A good chainsaw (same brands as the weed eater)
- A good helmet with a screened face guard and earmuffs for running the weed eater and saw
- A "pole saw" for pruning up high
- A good set of pruning shears with long handles
- A "fencing tool," available at most hardware stores
- A "fence stretcher" for stretching wire fence that remotely resembles some sort of car jack
- A heavy duty wheelbarrow with a wide tire
- A roto-tiller if you plan to raise a large garden, as this is your best option for weed control
- And, if you are rich, a four-wheeled ATV with a trailer, which will come in handy for scads of reasons!

For the most part, when you move to the country, the land will pretty much remain as it was when you moved there except for where you have cleared for fire protection and to clear your land for your uses. If it is pasture or some other agricultural use, it will have its own specific needs that are peculiar to it and all these diverse uses and their maintenance issues would vary in more ways than is practical to discuss here in this book. However, even then there will be parts of the property that will need the same maintenance as the rest.

If you stay on top of your weeds around fences, your drives, walkways, yard, and other such areas with weed-killing spray along with a "pre-emergent" that keeps seeds from sprouting once you have killed the weeds, you will find less work in removing these weeds with a weed eater. Spraying at the right time of year is very important, and you can contact your local agricultural extension for your county, the fertilizer company that sells the sprays, or some other such source to learn more about this in your area. If you don't want to use sprays, plan on using a weed eater much more often. With a riding mower in areas that are not rocky, you will find that no other tool can replace it.

Most of the other tools are pretty self-explanatory, and if you buy them, I promise you will thank me for recommending them. These are tools that sooner or later any country property owner will come to realize that they need and will use regularly in order to not work themselves to death! You will also find that using livestock, such as cows, horses, sheep, and goats, can be a great way to both keep your property looking groomed and to control the weeds, as well as keep your property clear for fire protection.

Any Last Thoughts to Help Me with My Country Property Experience?

Well, I covered most of them, but there are a couple of things that are good to know that I haven't mentioned.

When you build your home, you can install a modern "fire

sprinkler" system in the ceilings. In California, this has become required on nearly every country property. These sprinklers are not like the gaudy ones you see in some commercial building that stick down out of the ceiling. They are barely noticeable. A typical cost to add these to an 1800-square-foot house right now is about three thousand dollars, and it will save you monthly on your fire-insurance rates. It is important to note also that, when operating properly, the industry claims that there has never been a death of a human with one of these systems installed!

Get your shade trees in ASAP! Trees grow remarkably fast, several feet a year, and provide both comfort and energy savings, as well as increase your property's value, so get them in as soon as possible. Often folks will get around to planting trees after they have been in the property for five years or more, and had they planted their trees at first, they would already be reaping much of their benefit!

Be aware that there are many plants to use for landscaping that the deer will not eat. For instance, any plant with a "daisy" type flower, most bulb plants like daffodils and irises, and poisonous plants such as oleanders will be left alone by the deer and other critters. Your local nursery folks will be happy to help you out with such plants, and this will save you a lot of money and disappointment!

When you are fencing a large parcel, oftentimes you can use trees for both bracing your fence corner posts or use them as posts to stretch your fence along the way, and you will save yourself scads of money by not having to build elaborate corner posts and stretching points with posts and concrete, and because these big trees are not apt to budge, your fence will remain tighter, more secure for your animals, and better looking. Oftentimes I find the value of using these trees much more valuable than worrying about whether I am fencing perfectly straight so every inch of my property is perfectly fenced! I find trees that are on my property for sure, and as close to the property line as possible, and make nice long "runs" with the fencing so that portion is straight for a long distance. Each distance may vary, as I choose the "best" trees that are in line with and as close to my property as possible. I have never had a tree die yet due to this practice!

Another good fencing tip is to not use any higher of a fence than you need. Fencing is very expensive, and a lot of people have this fantasy when they move to the country that they are going to fence the world out with some seven-foot-high wire fence that costs four times as much as a normal chest-high fence that is needed to keep their horses, cows, and dogs in. These folks are fooling themselves, as if anyone wants in their property, which is unusual if you have any type of fence at all, they will bring along a ten-dollar pair of wire cutters and get in. Also, any so-determined person can easily climb any fence no matter how much barbed wire is on it. So, save yourself some money and fence for keeping your livestock in and not to keep folks out. Besides, that electric fence wire on your fence will deter most folks once they get a handful of it or a jolt to the "privates" as they straddle it to climb!

About the only time you need a high fence is to keep the deer out of your orchard or garden area. Fence these areas in separately as needed because, as I said, high fencing is very costly. I will mention here, too, that the more gates you have, the more times they will get left open, and the more you will be chasing your animals down the road. Gates are necessary, but minimize their use, especially in the perimeter fencing of your property.

Make it a point to have a load of pea gravel delivered, or at least bring home a pickup load. Pea gravel, when it is spread thinly on top of walkways and areas that you are tending to mill around in, is great to keep you, the dog, and the kids out of the mud, and this makes for less cleaning in the house, on the porches, and elsewhere. Pea gravel works best when spread in a layer just enough to cover the dirt, because if you get it too thick, you tend to bog down when walking in it and it makes it hard to roll a wheelbarrow and other such wheeled tools.

Set your dogs, livestock, and fowl up with automatic watering devices. These are typically very cheap and easy to install and will assure that your animals have water at all times without you having to worry about it. This will make your vacations easier on you and your caretaker. Having them all set up where they can have enough food for a couple of days is important, also, as it really frees you up when you can make a little weekend jaunt somewhere and not even have to worry much about a caretaker, as you aren't going to be gone long enough for something to die of thirst or hunger, anyway.

If you are going to raise chickens, do yourself and them a huge favor by making them a fully enclosed outdoor "run," so they can wander around in a reasonably large area and still be protected from the raccoons, foxes, skunks, and the rest of the predators. This includes having a fully enclosed wire roof. I have had chickens most of my life, and no matter where I lived, if I didn't shut them up almost every night, some varmint would come in and kill one or more of them. You get attached to them, and when they die just because you got too lazy or forgot to shut them up at night, it makes you feel like a real heel. That is why I mentioned keeping your animals a reasonable distance from the house.

While we are talking about chickens, I will mention that having a chicken coop design that allows you to gather the eggs without actually walking into the coop is a handy feature. Often you can build the "laying" boxes protruding out of the coop so you can lift the lid or you can rig up a sliding door to reach into the boxes inside. If you plan to let a chicken set on eggs to hatch them out, she has to be separated from the rest of the chickens. Chickens share nests when laying eggs, and will accumulate a nest full by laying one egg per day, which is what they lay, and once they get what they feel is the right amount (about a dozen), they will begin to sit on them non-stop, which begins the incubation period. If other chickens keep coming in and kicking her off the nest, share it with her, or occupy it when she is out grabbing a snack, and they lay in her nest during this incubation period, it causes problems, the biggest one being that it puts too many eggs in her nest so that she can't properly cover them with her body so none of them hatch.

Another little hint about chickens that a lot of people don't know is that chickens get avian lice, and this can really affect their egg laying. The feed store can help you with treating for these. Most people don't, and it is not a serious problem, but it is best to do if you want to have good egg production.

If you are in an area with snakes, guinea fowl will truly cut down on the snake population. The guinea hens are constantly on the prowl around your property and either kill the snakes or harangue them enough so they leave. Guinea hens can be loud and, just like peacocks, will make it a habit of jumping up on your and your guests' cars, eating the bugs off the windshields and laying new "hood ornaments"! They also have sharp toenails, and they will scratch the paint. I have seen some of my guests with that look in their eye, as if they wanted to strangle both the guinea hens and me when their cars got scratched!

If you are planning to raise sheep, goats, and such, you may want to invest in a "livestock guardian dog." These dogs are bred to watch over a herd of animals and fight to the death to protect them, and they will do so. They are usually very gentle and somewhat shy and could make a decent housedog. However, either plan to use them as a livestock guard or a housedog, as they cannot do both. If you get a livestock guard dog, you will introduce that dog as a puppy into the sheep herd and leave it with the herd. Make it a point for you, or any of your kids, or anyone, to not have contact with the dog except for feeding it once or twice a day. The dog should stay penned with the livestock with minimal human interaction so it bonds with them only and not your family, which it quickly will if you allow it. I know it is rough, especially when there is a little white, fluffy, sweet little butterball sitting down with the animals, but you MUST follow these rules or your dog is ruined for guarding the livestock.

Once it bonds with the sheep, it will not ever leave their sight, and the livestock will come to love it and know that it is their guardian angel. This dog will kill mountain lions, bobcats, other dogs, or anything that threatens its wards! It may later bond with you as well, but you will have no priority when it comes to the herd. My brother has a Marena Sheep Dog, and I have never seen anything like it. However, his buddy got one, and he didn't have his sheep yet and his kids loved it, and it bonded with his family and could care less about his herd! Another popular livestock guard dog is the Great Pyrenees. I am sure there are a few others, as well, but after seeing my brother's dog in action, why look a gift horse in the mouth!

If you have kids, get them involved in 4-H! You have the room for the hog pen, and 4-H is good for your kids to teach them responsibility and to occupy them in a healthy and wholesome way. The 4-H parents are usually very involved with their kids, and raising livestock together with your kids is a great experience that will allow you to bond even closer than you already are. I am of the school of thought that you can't keep drugs away from your kids; you have to keep your kids away from drugs, and living in the country and participating in 4-H is a great way to accomplish this, in part. Your kids will love the livestock shows at the county fairs, and you will, too. Ask in the local livestock feed store about how to contact your local group.

If you are in a fire-prone area, do not use weed eaters, mowers, and other equipment at times when one little spark can set off a fire that can destroy your entire neighborhood or more! Every year here in Northern California, many wildfires are started in this very way. The well-meaning landowner waits until a little too late in the spring and decides to remove the dead grass from around his property, as required by our fire regulations. Then the blade of their riding mower, push mower, or weed eater hits a rock and sends out a spark that scorches anywhere from a half an acre to thousands of acres.

Oftentimes, early in the mornings, there is moisture in the air and maybe even a little dew, and this presents a little window to clear dry grass and brush, but this window often disappears by ten in the morning. If there is any day with low humidity, no time is a good time to do this type of work.

Using a chainsaw for any reasons at such times is equally as risky. Even if you are a pyromaniac, you better realize that most of the time the government will hold you responsible for the costs of fighting any fire you start, which can run into the millions!

When you move to the country, you have to get your mail. Usually you see these little arched mailboxes with the little red pop-up flags on them at every driveway. This is one way to go, but there are better alternatives in this day and age of identity theft, let alone the fact that kids with baseball bats have a sport called "mailbox batting" that is popular in these country areas! It might be advisable to get a post office box in town near where you shop or work. Another popular alternative is the neighborhood mail boxes that have boxes for each neighbor, which are keyed for each person with one master key for the mail man in the rear. These are usually located at the entrance to a neighborhood, or close by it where it is safe to park and can be observed by one of the neighbors. These boxes seem to alleviate both theft and vandalism. Each neighbor usually chips in a share to purchase such a box, and any such box should be sized to anticipate more neighbors as vacant lots are occupied or because someone subdivides their land into more lots. You can contact your post office for information on purchasing these units.

Lastly, decide how you plan to deal with your trash. This is not a problem if you are in a neighborhood where the garbage man visits your home and empties it just like in town, but this is usually not the case in country properties. Oftentimes, the garbage man will pass by your driveway out on the county or private road because of your tight parking area or the dogs at your house, and you have to get your garbage down to that point. If your driveway is short and not uphill, this may be easy, but if not, it still has to get down there. Sometimes folks will leave their can down there and just put sacks in when they are driving past. This is true also if you and the neighbors have chipped in for a "dumpster" that is located at the beginning of your neighborhood. Still yet, some folks buy a trailer and fill it up for a month or two and then haul it to the landfill themselves. This is just something to think about.

In Closing...

It has been great spending a little time with you, and I hope you learned a lot about buying, selling, developing, and living on country property. Over the years, I have been asked most of these questions, and I wanted to just put it all in one organized place for all the folks that could benefit from me so doing. Now, every time somebody asks me questions about country property, all I have to do is give them the link on Amazon.com and let them know I will be awaiting their check in the mail!

I truly do enjoy living in the country, and I raised my two daughters, who are now nineteen and twenty-five years old, in the country, and I would not do it any other way if I had the chance. We grew up together as a family, and they grew up on good food, much of it that we raised, and we are all close today. Living the country lifestyle isn't for everyone, but there is a good chance that if you are even thinking about it that you are the type of person that will find the lifestyle as pleasant and enjoyable as my family and I did. Thanks for reading my book, my friend!

Made in the USA
San Bernardino, CA
27 April 2015